Freshwater Aquariums

Fish Keeping
Made Easy™

Freshwater Aquariums

Basic Aquarium Setup and Maintenance

David Alderton

BOWTIE™
P R E S S

Published in 2003 by BowTie Press
A Division of Fancy Publications
3 Burroughs, Irvine, CA 92618
www.bowtiepress.com
Fish Keeping Made Easy is an imprint of BowTie Press

Produced by Andromeda Oxford Limited
11–13 The Vineyard, Abingdon
Oxon OX14 3PX .
www.andromeda.co.uk

Project Director: Graham Bateman
Managing Editor: Shaun Barrington
Design: D and N DTP and Editorial Services
Editorial Assistant: Rita Demetriou
Picture Manager: Claire Turner
Production: Clive Sparling
Cartographer: Richard Watts
Indexer: Sheila Seacroft

Library of Congress Cataloging-in-Publication Data
Alderton, David, 1956-
    Freshwater aquariums : basic aquarium setup and maintenance/by David
        Alderton.
        p. cm.
    Includes bibliographical references (p.   ).
    ISBN 1-931993-11-4 (hardback : alk. paper)
    1. Aquariums. 2. Aquarium fishes. I. Title.
SF457 .A4284 2002
639.34—dc21   2002008846

Front cover: cardinal tetras (*Paracheirodon axelrodi*); *see* page 63.
(M. P. and C. Piednoir/Aquapress)
Page 2: banded dwarf cichlid *(Apistogramma bitaeniata)*.

Color origination by A.T. Color, Milan
Printed in France by Partenaires-Livres, Paris

Contents

Nature and Nurture

For many people, one of the most appealing aspects of fish keeping is that it is possible to replicate nature in the home, with both fish and living plants. Ironically, this naturalistic approach is easier to achieve today than in the past, thanks to the increasingly sophisticated technology now available.

Special lights, for example, help the growth of plants; and the increased efficiency of filtration systems means that maintaining good water quality for the fish themselves is much more straight-forward.

By understanding your fish and their behavior in the wild, and creating a more natural biotope for them, you are not simply bringing nature into your home, you are also lessening the likelihood of your fish falling ill. Ensuring that only compatible individuals are placed together and are not overcrowded effectively lessens the stress on them.

◔ The Belize rainforest, the original home of some of the most highly recommended fish for the first-time aquarist, the sword-tails (see page 81) and platies (page 82).

Understanding their natural spawning habits means that you can design the aquarium accordingly to increase the likelihood of successful breeding. If you are unaware of the need to incorporate some kind of shelter for cave-spawning cichlids, for example, then they will be deprived of the type of habitat where they will naturally spawn, making breeding unlikely. A number of different reproductive triggers apply in the wild. Failure to reproduce these in the home aquarium means that breeding becomes a hit-and-miss affair. In addition, failure to reproduce the different natural water conditions—acidity and alkalinity, softness and hardness—that fish experience in the wild will almost inevitably lead to problems.

Understanding your fish also means you will be able to see what is natural behavior, and what could indicate that not all is well with them. This will enable you to distinguish when a fish is likely to spawn for example, or is displaying signs of disease. Throughout this book insights into natural fish behavior, reflecting both their general and individual requirements, are to be found, with the aim of ensuring that your fish should stay healthy and live longer, in addition to increasing the likelihood that they will breed successfully.

This focus on natural fish, or piscine, behavior is not just of practical benefit. A deeper understanding of just why your fish are thriving is surely one of the joys of fish keeping. Hopefully, in reading this book, you will learn how to "read" your fish: which is to your benefit as well as theirs.

➊ This is "cardinal country," home to the cardinal tetra in northern Brazil (see page 63). Unsurprisingly, the advice for a cardinal tank includes subdued lighting, generous planting, and the addition of aquarium peat to the water.

CHAPTER 1

What are Fish?

Fish are the first vertebrates–animals with backbones–in the fossil record, with their origins extending back nearly 600 million years. A number of characteristics help to distinguish fish from other vertebrates. They breathe primarily by means of gills, through which they can extract oxygen from the water, and swim effectively by means of fins.

All fish are closely tied to water, being unable to live for any length of time on land, although a few of today's species can emerge on to land for short periods. Their original ancestors, however, were very different in appearance from any of the fish that are alive today. It is thought that the group developed from boneless creatures that simply sucked in water, and extracted food particles from it.

EVOLUTION

Fossil records indicate a number of different stages in the development of modern fish. The first major shift in their appearance was the development of external bony scales, which presumably gave them greater protection from predators. This change appears to have occurred in the late Cambrian period. Then, in a highly significant development for life on the planet, a bony framework began to develop in the body, creating the start of the vertebrate lineage.

The oldest example of a fish of this type has been unearthed in rocks dating back to the Early Ordovician, around 500 million years ago. Christened Aradaspis, this fish measured approximately 6in (15cm) in length, and swam in the region of what is present-day Australia. Being finless, it relied entirely on its tail for propulsion, and still sucked food into its mouth, having no jaws.

Another 80 million years passed before jaws developed during the Devonian period, appropriately in a group called the acanthodians, or spiny sharks. They also had a definite skeletal structure, with bone also providing support for their fins and protection, thanks to so-called dermal bone within the skin. Up until this stage, the backbone had been composed of cartilage. The overlaying of cartilage with bone ultimately gave way to fish whose skeletons were made entirely of bone. Today, bony fish have become

HOW JAWS DEVELOPED

The early fish had gills to extract oxygen from the water, and it is thought that the jaws developed from the first of the gill arches; teeth formed later from skin inside the mouth. The large gill slits associated with the first set of gill arches have since been reduced to tiny holes known as spiracles.

Anatomy of a fish.

The principal external features of a fish

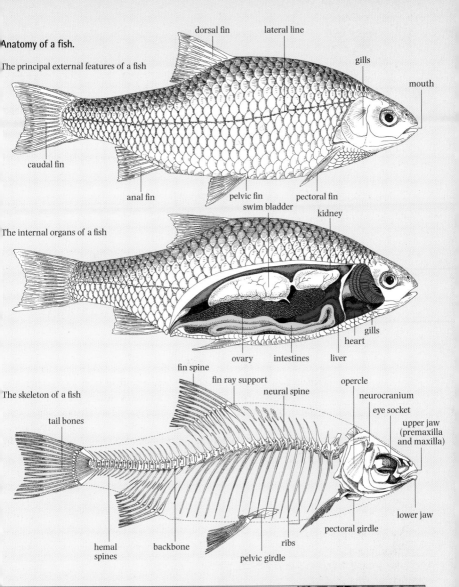

- dorsal fin
- lateral line
- gills
- mouth
- caudal fin
- anal fin
- pelvic fin
- pectoral fin

The internal organs of a fish

- swim bladder
- kidney
- gills
- heart
- ovary
- intestines
- liver

The skeleton of a fish

- fin spine
- fin ray support
- neural spine
- opercle
- neurocranium
- eye socket
- upper jaw (premaxilla and maxilla)
- tail bones
- lower jaw
- pectoral girdle
- hemal spines
- backbone
- ribs
- pelvic girdle

SHAPES OF TODAY

A number of the shapes typical of modern fish developed quite early in the evolutionary process. There were a number of flat-bodied fish, rather like today's discus (*Symphysodon* spp.), such as Platysomus, which inhabited both freshwater and marine environments. Platysomus lived for nearly 100 million years, from the Carboniferous through to the late Permian period.

Green discus (*S. aequifasciatus*).

⏷ The fossil record reveals that the remarkable coelacanth (*Latimeria chalumnae*), believed extinct and only rediscovered in 1938, has changed little since the time of the dinosaurs over 65 million years ago.

⏷ Scales protect the bodies of most fish, and different types of scale are used to classify different groups and sometimes describe species. This is a small-scale barb (*Labeo rahita*).

by far the most numerous group of vertebrates on the planet, with more than 20,000 recognized species.

RECENT LINEAGES

The bony fish, or teleosts, are the direct ancestors of modern groups of fish and first came to prominence during the late Triassic period, some 220 million years ago. Around 100 million years ago, the group underwent a rapid diversification. This led to a split, leading to fish that adapted to freshwater rather than marine environments. This new branch resembled modern fish more closely.

Hypsidoris, for example, closely resembled modern catfish, even to the extent of having recognizable barbels around its mouth, used for sensory purposes. It appears to have been numerous in freshwater lakes and rivers in the western part of North America. Hypsidoris also had protective spines on the pectoral fins. Fossilized skeletons, dating back 50 million years, reveal that it had good hearing, like its contemporary relatives. Hypsidoris was predatory by nature, hunting smaller fish and crustaceans like crayfish, and grew to about 8in (20cm) in length.

Unfortunately, it is impossible to tell the coloration or markings of any fish from their fossilized remains. However, it has been possible to work out quite accurately the likely lifestyle of fish, based on their physical features. Here the characteristics of modern fish, such as body shape and teeth, provide clues. The locality of fossil finds has also been helpful: where large numbers of fish of the same type have been discovered together, it is likely they lived in schools.

ANATOMY

Body protection

Most fish today have a body covering composed of scales, although the distribution and type of scales varies between individual fish. Overlapping so-called cycloid scales have a circular shape, overlapping each other to protect the body. They occur on many different types of fish, including cyprinids and cichlids, and can be very significant to ichthyologists, helping not only to age the fish but also to reveal much about the fish's growth rate.

Ctenoid scales are similar in terms of their overlapping patterning, but can be distinguished easily by the comblike edge apparent on close examination. Far less flexible in design are so-called ganoid scales, which are shaped like a trapezium. These are seen in older fish lineages, including the African reedfish *Erpetoichthys calabaricus*, which tend to be less active swimmers.

Catfish such as Corydoras have a different type of body covering, in the guise of bony plates. The young fry hatch without this type of protection; their skin becomes folded later, forming the basis for the plates. They are relatively large, and their shape is clearly visible. Although providing effective protection, these bony plates are quite inflexible, compared with scales. As a result, they reduce the fish's maneuverability and agility. Because such catfish are covered in these bony plates they are often described as being armored. In fact, the plates are so thick that they would block the underlying functioning of the lateral line (see page 15), cutting out vibrations from the water. The lateral line, however, still functions by means of pores between the plates. Corydoras catfish are relatively slow swimmers, in common with other bony plated fish.

🔼 Catfish can only swim relatively slowly, because of their inflexible body covering of bony plates rather than scales. This is the frogmouth catfish, (*Chaca chaca*), a night hunter.

Respiration

A fish typically has around 185 different bones in its skull, providing support and protection for vital processes such as respiration via the gills. The gill flap or operculum, lying near the back of the head on each side of the body, needs bones as well as muscles to operate effectively. The gill flap is not simply used for breathing or swallowing: gill flaps can be flared for display purposes or as a threat to a would-be rival.

How the gills work

As the fish starts to suck water into its mouth at the start of the respiratory cycle, the gills are closed off by the operculum or gill cover. The water then passes across the network of blood vessels that comprise the gills. It is here that oxygen diffuses into the blood returning from the body, while carbon dioxide, accumulated from the body's internal processes, now passes out of the blood into the water, in a process known as gaseous exchange. The gills themselves have a large surface area, to facilitate gaseous exchange, ensuring maximum contact between the gills and the water. The structure of the gills provides a simple way to distinguish between bony fish and their surviving cartilaginous relatives. These more ancient relatives rely on a series of gill slits on the side of the head, although the flow of water occurs over the gills themselves in a similar way.

Lungfish (*Protopterus* genus) can actually survive by burrowing into the mud when their pools dry up.

The fish's heart, located just behind the gills near the throat, consists of four chambers. It is responsible for pumping deoxygenated blood to the nearby gills, and then oxygenated blood returning to the ventricle out around the body.

Fins

The shape and structure of the fish's fins are important in giving practical clues not just to its classification but also to its lifestyle. Most fish have seven fins on their bodies. There are the paired pectoral and pelvic fins on each side of the body, with the pectoral fins located behind the gills. The actual positioning of the pelvic fins is a more variable feature between the different groups of fish, although the anal fin always occurs behind the pelvic fins. The powerful caudal fin, sometimes described as the tail fin, is located at the end of the body. This fin is developed and used to varying degrees among species. Fish with a decidedly serpentine body shape, such as the kuhli loach (*Pangio kuhli*), rely as much on their body movement as that of their caudal fin to provide them with their propulsive power.

Another relatively large fin, known as the dorsal, is located in the midline and runs down the back. The dorsal fin in a number of aquarium fish such as the sailfin molly (*Poecilia latipinna*) is often naturally enlarged and may be used for display purposes. There can also be sharp spines here, to deter predators, as for various catfish, but generally, the dorsal fin serves as a stabilizer. It can help to slow the fish down: if the end of the fin nearest the tail is curled, the drag factor increases. Some fish, notably the characins, may also display a small adipose fin behind the dorsal, reinforcing its action.

The pectoral fins act as stabilizers, an important function when water is forced out of the operculum. They can also provide propulsive power, being especially pronounced in fish that will leap out of

◑ Body shape differs widely even between related fish, varying from flat to cylindrical, as shown by Endicher's polypterus (*Polypterus endicheri endicheri*), a relative of the lungfish.

IMPACT OF SELECTION

The shape of the fins has been altered by selective breeding, especially in the case of the goldfish (*Carassius auratus*) and livebearers such as the guppy (*Poecilia reticulata*), so that their fins may not function as effectively as in the wild. This may have implications in aquarium surroundings if such fish are less able to reach food first.

Guppy (*Poecilia reticulata*).

❯ Black molly (*Poecilia latipinna*). Ornamental varieties of fish are judged in shows partly on the shape of their fins.

❮ The fins work together with remarkable precision, even allowing fish to hover in the water at times, as may occur during spawning. There are about 35 species in the genus *Poecilia* and hybridization sometimes makes identification tricky.

the water, such as hatchetfish (*Gasteropelecus* and *Carnegiella* spp.). In contrast, the pelvic fins help to maintain the fish's position in the water, allowing it to swim in a level line, and protect against pitching.

The anal fin, located behind this opening, also has a stabilizing effect. It is especially well developed in some tetras. And in the case of male livebearers, it has evolved into a tubelike structure called the gonopodium in males, allowing them to mate directly with females.

Sensory inputs

The ways in which fish naturally orientate themselves can be significant in aquarium surroundings. Many fish keepers worry about keeping blind cave fish (*Astyanax fasciatus mexicanus*) in an aquarium alongside other fish, fearing they will be at a disadvantage here, as a result of their lack of sight. These unusual fish have a very restricted distribution in the wild, confined to a network of caves in Mexico. It is believed that a population of these fish became trapped in this dark environment, evolving along different lines from those of their ancestral relatives living in neighboring rivers.

⬇ The lateral line runs down both sides of the body. It is difficult to make out even if the fish is semitransparent, like the Indian glassfish, (*Chanda ranga*)!

Blind cave fish have developed unique characteristics in response to their new habitat, where the darkness has made their eyesight irrelevant. Although their fry still hatch with normal eyes, these soon become covered with skin as they grow, so they can no longer function. Furthermore, they have also lost their pigmentation, giving them a semitransparent pinkish glow.

If kept in the company of other fish in an aquarium, however, blind cave fish display no apparent disadvantages, either in terms of avoiding obstacles or indeed obtaining food. Part of this is due the presence of the lateral line, which is a jelly-filled canal running the length of the body, approximately halfway down each side. Lying just beneath the skin, it acts rather like an underwater echo locator, picking up changes in pressure caused by the movement of water back off obstacles around the fish. This causes vibrations in the canals, which are then transmitted up to the brain. The sensory input allows the fish to interpret its position accordingly, and swim safely without colliding with obstacles.

The same system also warns of possible predators approaching, allowing the blind cave fish to take evasive action. As a further adaptation to their darkened world, these fish may also possess a heightened sense of smell, since not only can they find food easily, but they may even locate and eat their own eggs after spawning in the aquarium.

Power play

Approximately 250 fish are known to be capable of generating electrical currents in their bodies. Some species use this power to stun and capture prey, but the majority rely on this ability simply to orientate themselves. It is especially common in fish found in stretches of water that are either murky or choked with vegetation. Sight would be of relatively limited value in such an environment.

One of the most popular groups of aquarium fish using electricity for this purpose are the elephant-nosed fish (*Gnathonemus* spp.) originating from parts of Africa. They are so called because of their sensitive trunklike snout, which they use to seek worms and other aquatic live food in the substrate. Elephant-nosed fish are quite social by nature and it appears that within a small group, they may be able to identify each other by their electrical outputs. The actual voltage that they generate is exceedingly weak and can only be measured with sensitive equipment. By surrounding themselves with a force field of this type, these fish are also able to detect the approach of a possible predator, or indeed static objects such as rocks in their vicinity. Elephant-nosed fish need to be accommodated in an aquarium where the lighting level is very subdued, mimicking that of their natural habitat.

Fish that rely on their electrical power to hunt are usually large: adult electrical catfishes (*Malapturus* spp.), for example, typically measure 24–39in (0.6–1m). Size alone makes them unsuitable as aquarium occupants, but these fish pose an electrical danger: they can generate an output of more than 450 volts!

Electricity-generating fish actually have three different electrical organs located in different parts of their bodies. Like elephant-nosed fish, they rely on a passive electrical output to orientate themselves; this electricity-sensing organ is near the tail. The main electrical impulse for stunning prey is discharged from the head and top of the body, with a secondary output being released from the underside of the body.

⬆ Electric catfish (*Malepterurus electricus*). These fish are even dangerous to people.

HABITATS

The stocking density within an aquarium is not just influenced by the number and size of the fish. It also needs to reflect the areas of the tank that they will occupy, in order to avoid conflicts. Even if you are not familiar with a particular species, you can actually tell much about its lifestyle from its appearance.

A community of compatible medium-sized fish. When selecting fish for a community aquarium, consider the full depth of the water column. It is possible to create activity in all zones.

Top of the tank

Fish that occupy the upper part of an aquarium have a relatively straight back as well as curved underparts, as exemplified by the hatchetfish (family Gasteropelecidae). These South American fish remain close to the surface, often lurking out of sight here under aquatic vegetation. They are very alert, however, darting out to grab any insects that break the surface of the water. Their upturned mouths help them with these attacks. Hatchetfish in particular must always be kept in covered aquariums. Otherwise, they are likely to leap out of the tank, with potentially fatal consequences. Plants on the surface are also important, providing them with cover because they are quite nervous fish by nature.

Bottom dwellers

At the other extreme, Corydoras catfish (*Corydoras* spp.), originating from the same part of the world, have very flat underparts, enabling them to hug the bottom of the tank. Their mouths, located on the underside of their heads, indicate that they will seek their food on the floor of the aquarium. Inhabiting waters where visibility is often poor, these catfish have small sensory projections around their mouths, called barbels, to help them find food. Catfish represent one of the most diverse families of aquarium fish. Other catfish species are far less placid than Corydoras. A more streamlined body shape helps their swimming; their much longer barbels indicate a predatory nature. Since catfish in general are nocturnal, becoming more active when the lights are switched off in an aquarium, do not be fooled by such fish when they seem quite placid during the daytime. They will be transformed into highly efficient hunters at night, preying on smaller tank companions, and so must not be housed in the company of vulnerable fish.

The mid-zone

If you are setting up an aquarium for Amazonian fish, with hatchetfish occupying the top and Corydoras catfish the bottom, then mid-zone-dwelling tetras are ideal companions. This habitat preference is reflected by their shape, which is largely symmetrical, with their mouth being located centrally. Tetras have well-muscled bodies and powerful tails to enable them to swim strongly. Such fish often live in schools, an effective defense because a hunter finds it harder to target an individual within a group. In addition, the bright, contrasting flashes of color on a tetra may act as a further source of confusion to a would-be predator.

CHAPTER 2

Setting Up an Aquarium

Few hobbies are more relaxing than fish keeping, and thanks to modern technology it is easier than ever to set up and maintain a freshwater aquarium. You need to consider various factors at the outset, however, not least your intended choice of fish. This will affect the size of the tank, and also its decor. You might also find it preferable to keep certain types of fish, because of the chemical composition of your local water supply.

ⓘ BAD DESIGNS

Bear in mind that more elaborate aquarium setups are harder to keep clean, particularly if algal growth develops in connecting tubes. Never choose tanks that have been converted into dual-purpose items of furniture, such as lamps or tables of any type. These can be subjected to major changes in temperature or vibration, which will be transmitted into the water and will almost certainly distress the fish.

Although most people still favor a tradi-tional rectangular aquarium design, a number of different styles are available today. You can choose triangular tanks, or even separate interconnecting tanks, joined by a clear tube through which the fish can swim back and forth. This will not create any problems for the fish themselves, although it may restrict your choice, because clearly, you cannot choose any species that is likely to outgrow the diameter of the tunnel. Such a setup allows you to keep fish that become more territorial as they grow older, since they will be effectively separated in this environment.

SIZE

One of the most significant features of a tank is its surface area; it is here that gaseous exchange occurs. The carbon dioxide produced by the fish, and to a lesser extent by the plants, will pass out here, with oxygen diffusing into the water. The water in a tropical aquarium actually holds less oxygen than a coldwater tank, although this variation is of relatively little significance because coldwater fish generally require more oxygen to drive their body processes.

STOCKING CALCULATION

Allow 30sq in (194sq cm) of surface area per inch (2.5cm) of cold-water fish (length of fish minus tail), compared with 12sq in (77sq cm) for tropicals when calculating the size. You can calculate this surface area figure easily, simply by multiplying the length of the aquarium by its width.

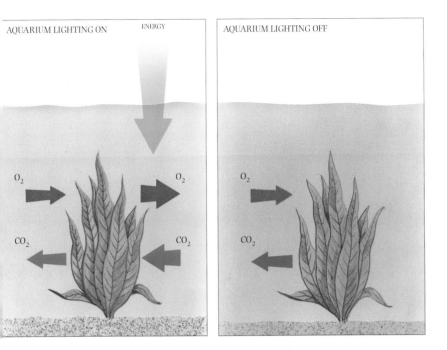

AQUARIUM LIGHTING ON   ENERGY

AQUARIUM LIGHTING OFF

O_2

O_2

O_2

CO_2

CO_2

CO_2

Living plants have an overall beneficial effect on the level of oxygen dissolved in the water. In well-lit surroundings, the plants will draw carbon dioxide from the water, releasing oxygen as part of a process called photosynthesis. With the lights off, photosynthesis stops but plant respiration continues. That's why plants used to be, and sometimes still are, removed from hospital wards at nighttime! But the net effect of respiration and photosynthesis is a definite oxygen plus.

AVOID OVERSTOCKING

The surface area of a tank is critical when deciding upon the number of fish that can be kept in the aquarium. Bear in mind that many aquarium fish, ranging from goldfish to angelfish (*Pterophyllum* spp.), are sold as young stock, and can grow much larger. Avoid overstocking at the outset so that the fish will not be overcrowded within the first few months. Overcrowding often leads to bullying, in addition to health problems.

Angelfish (*Pterophyllum scalare*).

⊕ Glass aquaria are made of panels, held together by special silicone sealant, but this does not mean that their shapes have to be square or rectangular. Beware with more unusually shaped tanks, however, because it will be harder to obtain undergravel filter plates for them.

MODERN TANK DESIGN

The more elaborate aquarium designs are made from acrylic rather than glass. Acrylic tanks, unlike glass tanks, are molded and have no joints. Since they are lighter and easier to move, acrylic tanks have become especially popular in the design of complete starter aquariums. Remember, though, that an acrylic tank is still delicate. If it is dropped, it will crack readily, even if does not actually shatter like glass.

When acrylic tanks were introduced, the sides also used to discolor quite easily, becoming yellowish, but this problem has now been largely overcome. Nevertheless, the sides can be scratched quite easily, so check before buying that there is no obvious damage here, particularly in the case of a secondhand tank. Apart from being unsightly, such scratches can be highlighted by algal growth within them.

Glass tanks are assembled using a special silicone sealant. It bonds strongly to form a waterproof seal but still remains flexible so that it will not dry out and leak like putty, which was formerly used in building tanks. Check that the sealant is evenly spread over the joints where the sheets of glass meet, to ensure that they are well bonded. Water imposes considerable force on the aquarium, and in the case of glass tanks over 24in (60cm) long, you should fix supporting struts across the tank to provide extra support.

The plastic borders around the edges of an aquarium will protect its corners, which are especially vulnerable to damage in transit. This type of edging also helps to give the aquarium a more attractive appearance.

Getting the tank home

When taking a glass aquarium home, lay it flat on a blanket. Fold this over the vulnerable ends, to guard against damage, and wedge it in place in your vehicle so that it cannot slide. If you are buying a secondhand tank, always ensure that it is empty before moving it.

Wash the tank out thoroughly before putting it in place, even if it is new. Any dust could cloud the water, and microscopic spicules of glass could also pose a threat to the fish. The simplest way to rinse the tank is to lay it carefully on one side outdoors, so that it cannot fall over, and wash out the interior with a hose. This method also lets you know whether a glass tank has a leak. Again, however, you need to take care when handling the tank, to ensure that it is not accidentally damaged, bearing in mind that glass slides through the fingers very easily when it is wet. Wipe around the outside with a clean cloth, to remove any water splashes. Do not use any chemicals: any residues could harm the tank occupants.

If you buy a glass tank bonded by silicone, you should also get a sheet of polystyrene corresponding to the dimensions of the tank. Put this in place first, as a base support. It will absorb any irregularities in the surface beneath; these could otherwise cause the tank to leak once it is full.

ⓘ SECONDHAND TANKS

Secondhand tanks and equipment can represent a significant saving compared to purchasing new items. But try to ascertain the fate of the fish, because there is a risk that they may have succumbed to illness. It is important to see the system operating if possible, bearing in mind that both heaterstats and lights have a limited lifespan. It may be better to discard any substrate in the tank and simply clean the aquarium thoroughly with a special aquarium disinfectant.

Do not be tempted to use an ordinary household disinfectant, however, because this is likely to be toxic to the fish. Use aquarium disinfectant solution to wash the heaterstat, filter components, and any other equipment (but obviously not the lighting) that will have been directly exposed to the water. Follow the instructions for use carefully.

SITING YOUR TANK

You will need to decide at the outset where the aquarium is to be sited, because even a relatively small 7.9-gallon (30-liter) tank will be very heavy to move once it is full, with each gallon of water weighing 8 pounds (3.6kg). If you make a mistake and then need to move the aquarium, you will have to empty it first. This process is time-consuming as well as being stressful for the fish.

It is a good idea to choose a room where you sit down to relax, so you can enjoy watching the fish in comfort. Hallways are not ideal, because the temperature here can fluctuate more significantly than elsewhere in the home, affecting unheated aquariums in particular. More significantly perhaps, an aquarium is also at risk of being damaged more easily in this location by people passing through, carrying a variety of objects.

A more secluded location is safer, but avoid siting it next to a radiator because this will also lead to fluctuations in the water temperature. Similarly, never place an aquarium in a window or anywhere where it will be exposed to direct sunlight for any length of time. This is not only because of the need to maintain a relatively constant water temperature, but also because exposure to bright light could trigger unwanted algal growth. This could cause unsightly green deposits to form inside the tank.

The electrical arrangements within the room may also have an impact on the location of the aquarium, since you need to be able to reach power points to run equipment such as heaters and filtration systems, without trailing electrical cords out over the floor. Although there may be three or more electrical items within the aquarium, these can often be wired into a power strip, so that only one power point is needed, but this cannot be repeatedly disconnected to operate other household appliances.

Do not place the aquarium next to a television or stereo system because you could spill water on to the unit when cleaning the tank. More significantly, however,

⊕ Larger aquariums built into a cabinet can be purchased. They come in a variety of designs and finishes, so that they can match well with any existing decor.

the sound waves will be transmitted through the water and this vibration could prove stressful for the fish. Vibration will register via the jelly-filled canals running up each side of the body, comprising the lateral line (see page 15).

CABINETS

Larger aquariums in particular are often available built into a cabinet, which can serve as a piece of furniture. Most manufacturers offer such cabinets in a range of designs and wood finishes, ranging from the contemporary to the more traditional, so that it is not difficult to obtain a unit that merges well into any setting. A cabinet is often ideal for an alcove, and provides a more attractive option than a tank stand, albeit at a significantly greater cost.

Stands consist of a metal support for the tank to raise it to just below eye-level. There is usually a lower shelf where ornaments can be placed, integrating this into the room. However, a stand, unlike a cabinet, will not conceal the electrical wires trailing from the aquarium. Nor will it be possible to hide an external power filter for example, which can be located in the base of the cabinet. You can tape the cabling in place down the back of a stand to conceal its presence.

The tank itself will need to be level, especially in the case of a glass aquarium. Otherwise, there will be extra pressure from the water on the joints, which could ultimately leak. The polystyrene underlay will not serve to support the sides in this respect, only the base. Always check the positioning of the aquarium with a level before filling it. If it does need adjusting because of a sloping floor, then you will need to provide additional support underneath the stand, perhaps with a wooden coaster.

THE SUBSTRATE

The base covering chosen for the tank, known as the substrate, is important because it can have effects on the water chemistry. It will also affect the way that we see the fish, because pale-colored gravel effectively drains their color, causing them to appear paler than normal.

Coarse aquarium gravel is better than sand in most cases, particularly where an undergravel filter is being used (see pages 30–1), because this provides an ideal basis for the development of bacterial colonies to break down the fish's waste. In addition, it is less likely to enter the fish's gills through the gill

⊙ Killifish aquarium with a black substrate, and a foam sponge filter. Aquarium gravel can affect the look of the fish by its color, either enhancing their attractiveness by contrast or making them look "washed out." Its composition may impact directly on the water chemistry as well.

GRAVEL PREPARATION

Whichever form of gravel you choose, it is still important to clean it thoroughly, because even if it has been prewashed, it will not be free of dirt. This in turn will cloud the water, and is also likely to form an unpleasant scum on the surface of the tank once it is filled. Start therefore by tipping the gravel into a clean bucket, and allow it to stand overnight in a solution of aquarium disinfectant. This should kill off any potential disease-causing organisms that could harm the fish.

In brackish-water aquaria, a coarser, more calcareous substrate can be used.

Finally, before tipping the gravel into the aquarium, rinse it off thoroughly in small batches using a colander, to ensure that it is completely clean. If you are using an undergravel filter, place this on the floor of the tank, before the gravel is added on top. In order to function effectively as a filter bed, the gravel here should be piled up to a depth of at least 3in (7.5cm).

⊙ NATURAL BEHAVIOR

There are a few groups of fish for which a gravel base in the aquarium is not ideal, and so a different type of filtration method will also be advisable. This is especially true in the case of elephant-nosed fish (*Gnathonemus* spp.), whose trunklike snouts probe for food. Avoid using coral sand (which is popular for use in marine tanks) in this case, however, because its high limestone content will affect the water chemistry. You should use silver sand instead. It is not necessary to cover the floor entirely with this material. A covering of sand can be laid on top of a bed of gravel, allowing the fish to root about in the substrate. Prepare the sand in the same way, but wash it in a fine sieve rather than a colander.

Elephant-nosed fish (*Gnathonemus petersi*) probing for food.

The substrate-spawning killifish (see page 85) are another group that needs an alternative to gravel as the aquarium base. They typically lay their eggs in the mud at the bottom of the temporary pools that they inhabit. They are normally provided with a floor covering comprised of special aquarium peat, which is tipped into the tank and left to become saturated so that it sinks. A gentle filtration system rather than a power filter will avoid disturbing this particular floor covering.

cover or operculum, and cause irritation here, compared with fine sand. This is true in particular of fish that regularly dig in the substrate, such as some cichlids as well as goldfish.

Packaged gravel consists of particles of fairly even size, so there are usually no tiny chips here, and if it has been prewashed, this makes it less dusty as well. But you need to check the type of gravel. While granite is inert, any gravel containing limestone will affect the water chemistry. This is because the calcium in the limestone will gradually dissolve into the water, causing it to become harder (see page 45). Hard water can be harmful for the many aquarium fish that inhabit areas of soft water in the natural state.

Aside from natural gravel, there are now a number of artificially colored shades available. When viewed in isolation, these may appear attractive, but again many colored gravels also detract from the color of the fish themselves. Red gravel, for example, dulls the appearance of red swordtails (*Xiphophorus helleri*). Colored gravel does not work if you are seeking to create a naturalistic setting in the aquarium. There is also a risk that the dye may sometimes leach out into the water. Allow about 2.2 pounds (1kg) of gravel per 1.2 gallons (4.5 liters) of aquarium volume.

HEATING

Some fish, typically goldfish, can be kept in an aquarium without the need for any heating at normal room temperature. Other fish too, notably those from more temperate parts of the world, such as white cloud mountain minnows (*Tanichthys albonubes*) originating from China, will usually thrive in similar surroundings. Water temperature is important because fish that are kept in relatively warmer surroundings than normal may tend to breed faster but can have a somewhat shorter lifespan on average based on studies with guppies (*Poecilia reticulata*).

Most tropical fish aquariums should be heated to approximately 77°F (25°C), with a single unit, known as a heaterstat, commonly being used, though this temperature will not be ideal for tropical species. Both the heater and thermostat are combined in a tightly sealed glass casing, with external suckers holding the tube in place on the side of the aquarium. These units are usually supplied ready-calibrated,

ⓘ OPERATING CARE

Heaterstats in general are quite long-lived and robust, but they must be kept submerged at all times when in operation. Always switch off the heaterstat for a few moments before carrying out any partial water change that could leave it temporarily exposed. If lifting the unit out of the aquarium, bear in mind that the glass itself is likely to be hot as well. Luckily, most designs now incorporate a safety switch–off so that if the unit becomes dislodged in the aquarium and floats to the surface, it will turn itself off automatically without causing any damage.

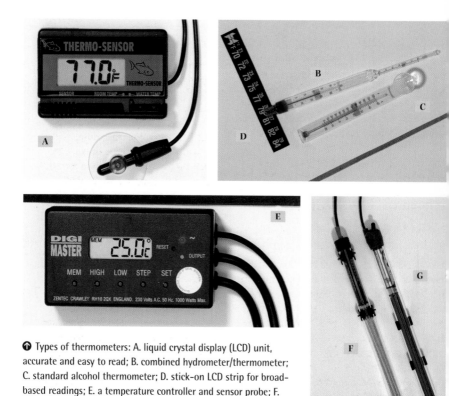

🔵 Types of thermometers: A. liquid crystal display (LCD) unit, accurate and easy to read; B. combined hydrometer/thermometer; C. standard alcohol thermometer; D. stick-on LCD strip for broad-based readings; E. a temperature controller and sensor probe; F. and G. heaters with built-in thermostats.

and are more reliable than traditional designs based on bimetallic strips, where the metal expands as it becomes warmer, switching off the heater, and then contracts as it cools, reactivating the heating unit again. This constant cycle of contraction and expansion works well at first, but can lead to a risk of fusion, so that the heater is not turned off once the water has reached the required temperature.

As a precautionary measure, it is worthwhile acquiring an aquarium alarm, which will alert you to any dramatic rise in water temperature caused by any failure of the heating system. It is a useful precaution to replace heaterstat units about every three years. They may have started to fail by then in any event, although some will continue to operate quite satisfactorily over a much longer period.

If you live in a part of the world where the weather is usually warm, it may not be necessary to have any form of heating even in a tropical fish aquarium, but it will still be important to monitor the water temperature. This can be done by means of an aquarium thermometer. Traditional designs are filled with colored alcohol, and attached inside the tank with a rubber sucker. They have been largely superseded today by flat digital thermometers in the form of a thin strip, stuck on the outside of the tank. These are very easy to read, but they will not be reliable unless they are stuck firmly against the glass. In addition, bear in mind that children find these fascinating, once they realize they can make the color bands change when they touch them, and this can be very misleading if the cause of the change is not appreciated.

⊘ AGGRESSION

Especially with large and potentially aggressive fish, such as the bigger cichlids, it is not necessarily a good idea to place the heater within the aquarium. Instead, use a heat pad that fits below the aquarium. These are available in various sizes. Also, since they are controlled via a tank thermostat, they are particularly useful when you need to lower the water level while maintaining the warm temperature. This may be the case in a spawning tank.

LIGHTING

Illumination above the aquarium is a very important feature, both to show the natural beauty of the fish, and also to encourage the growth of plants within the aquarium. Plants depend on aquarium lighting just as they would on sunlight outdoors to provide them with the energy to drive the reaction known as photosynthesis. However, not all lights emit light of the correct wavelength, which should correspond to that of sunlight itself. Ordinary incandescent bulbs, for example, will provide illumination, but they will not enable aquarium plants to grow and thrive. These bulbs are not really recommended for use above aquariums in any event, because aside from creating a yellowish cast, they are also short lived when hung on their sides or vertically downward.

⊙ Choosing the correct lighting for the aquarium is important not just in order to see the fish at their best, but also to encourage healthy plant growth.

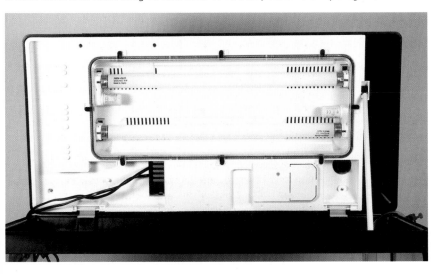

In order to see the fish at their best and encourage natural plant growth, choose special fluorescent tubes; these emit light from the red and blue part of the spectrum, corresponding to that of natural sunlight. The other major advantage of these lights over incandescent bulbs is that they produce virtually no heat, and so will not have any effect on the water temperature.

These so-called "natural lights" are available in various lengths, corresponding to the sizes of aquarium hoods, where they can be fitted securely, free from the risk of being splashed. The connectors in the hoods accommodate the prongs at the end of the light, and if these are broken or otherwise damaged, the tube will not work properly. The tube is clamped in place by plastic connectors, and there is a reflector panel above to direct the light back down into the aquarium.

🔽 The dark marbled hatchetfish (*Carnegiella strigata fasciata*) is one example of a fish that requires heavily tannin-stained water and subdued lighting conditions. This fish is used to the dark, thickly vegetated stretches of the Amazon basin and Guianas. Its eggs are deposited among the feathery roots of floating plants.

A daily cycle

Do not to keep the aquarium permanently illuminated, because the fish too have a biorhythm that responds to changing levels of illumination. Once they are established in the aquarium, you can turn off the lights both in the tank and the room simultaneously, but initially, switch off the lighting above the tank first and wait for five or ten minutes before doing so in the room itself. This will give the fish time to adjust. If they are plunged into sudden darkness, they may panic, swimming wildly around the tank and injuring themselves.

If you go back into the room after it has been dark for some time, and switch on a light, you are likely to notice that brightly colored fish in particular are paler in color than usual. This is as a result of changes in the pigment cells of their body, with fish sleeping for short periods at this stage. Fish that tend to hide away during the day will be more conspicuous.

Other lighting systems

In more specialist tanks, particularly those where growing plants are dominant, there are different lighting choices. Suspended lights of various types can be used in these surroundings. Their rays penetrate very

effectively in relatively deep tanks. Unfortunately, they do not fit into a typical hood, and so the level of evaporation from aquariums of this type will be high, along with an increased risk of airborne pollution, which could poison the fish. It is particularly important that chemical sprays are not used in the room where the aquarium is sited. The lights themselves are expensive to buy and running costs too are relatively high. They also tend to generate a lot of heat, which means they are definitely not recommended for use in aquariums housing fish that spawn at the water surface. So-called "cool" spotlights are better in this respect than metal halide or high-pressure mercury lights.

DARKENED ENVIRONMENTS

Some aquarium fish, such as blind cave fish (*Astyanax mexicanus*), do not originate from areas of sunlight or clear water. In these cases, it is possible to screen the surface with floating plants, so the light reaching the lower parts of the aquarium is more dappled. Alternatively, it may be better to abandon any hope of growing aquarium plants, and use plastic substitutes, or even other types of tank decor to create a natural environment.

FILTRATION

Within most aquariums, fish are living at significantly higher densities than they do in the wild. Furthermore, the aquarium is a closed system. There is no rain, for example, to dilute the water in the tank, and therefore the fish's waste. Even so, the natural cycle of decomposition does occur, and will be assisted by the presence of living plants in the aquarium. This is thanks to the beneficial bacteria that utilize the relatively toxic ammonia produced by the fish. The bacteria break it down through stages to nitrite and then relatively harmless nitrate, which can be used by the plants as a fertilizer, providing them with a valuable source of nitrogen. This is often described as the nitrogen cycle. In the absence of aquarium plants, however, the level of nitrate can build up. It is then taken up by microscopic plants known as algae, which would otherwise be competing with the aquarium plants for the nitrate in the water, and this is more likely to cause an overgrowth of algae as a result.

One of the problems that arise soon after setting up an aquarium, especially if it is heavily stocked with fish at the outset, is that

An undergravel filtration system in operation, with gravel in place. A non-return valve prevents water running into the pump, which must be left running constantly.

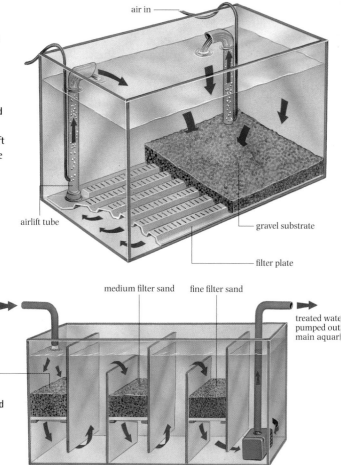

○ A tank fitted with a conventional-flow undergravel filter. In this system, water is drawn down through the filter bed (substrate) and returned via the airlift tube to the top of the aquarium.

air in

airlift tube

gravel substrate

filter plate

water flows by gravity from main aquarium

medium filter sand

fine filter sand

treated water pumped out main aquarium

coarse filter sand

○ A gravity-fed rapid sand filter. This unit comprises a series of compartments containing trays, through which the tank water is passed. A superior (and expensive) filter setup like this is not usually seen in the home aquarium— until, perhaps, you really catch the aquarist bug! A secondary tank like this can be hidden in a cabinet like the one on page 22.

the population of beneficial bacteria will be relatively low. Therefore the ammonia level is likely to remain high, threatening the health of the fish. It therefore helps to add a culture of beneficial bacteria when setting up the tank. This will speed the development of their colonies, which form the basis for the development of an undergravel filter.

Water containing the fish's waste in solution is drawn down through the filter bed, comprising particles of gravel where these bacteria are located, and broken down, assuming the filter is working effectively. The bacteria themselves depend on oxygen, and water must have free passage through the stones, which is why gravel particles are better than any type of sand as a medium for an undergravel filter. Over time however, the gravel may not only become compacted but mulm may block the spaces between the

MECHANICAL FILTRATION

MECHANICAL PLUS
CHEMICAL FILTRATION

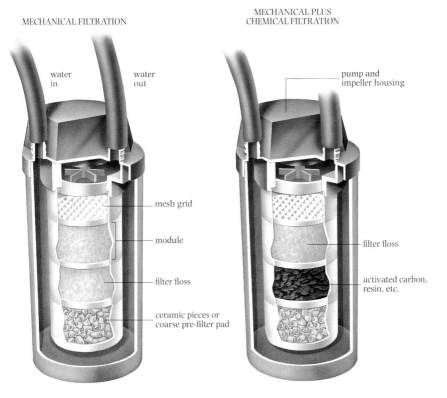

water
in

water
out

pump and
impeller housing

mesh grid

module

filter floss

filter floss

activated carbon,
resin, etc.

ceramic pieces or
coarse pre-filter pad

stones, so that regular cleaning of the filter bed with a gravel cleaner is essential to keep the system working effectively.

Filter types

There are several different types of filtration used in aquariums;
often more than one is used in the same tank. Power filters of various types are especially recommended where large fish such as
goldfish are being kept, because they will cope well with their
waste. Smaller designs of power filter can be fitted directly inside
the aquarium, drawing the water through the filter by means of a
pump and impeller unit. These are very effective filters, in terms of
the volume of water drawn through the foam cartridge lying at
their core. However, they do represent a hazard to young fry, which
may be unable to counter the current and so end up being sucked
into the filter.

External power or canister filters of this type take water from the
aquarium and return it once it has passed through the different lay-
ers within the canister. They are more suited to larger aquariums.
Depending on the design, canister filters will clean the water in

● Two ways to
utilize a canister
filter. These models
use internal clip-
together modules,
each holding a
different medium.

several ways. There is often an area of foam
or filter media in the unit to trap dirt particles: this process is known as mechanical filtration. In addition, however, beneficial
bacteria also accumulate in this filter medium, undertaking what is described as biological filtration.

Other material may be specifically included
in a separate chamber within the filter to
encourage this process. Ceramic chips, for
example, have a large surface area to support
bacterial colonies. Finally, there can be items
such as activated charcoal, which has the
ability to remove ammonia directly from the
water by a process known as adsorption, with
the ammonia molecules being trapped in the
carbon, or by the use of another chemical
called zeolite. This action is described as
chemical filtration, and within a canister fil-
ter, all three types of filtration may take place. Chemical filtration is
particularly important in a new tank to maintain water quality, before
biological filtration is fully effective. It typically takes perhaps six
weeks for a biological filter to reach its optimal level of function, and
before that happens, there will be a measurable buildup of nitrogenous waste in the tank, possibly endangering the health of the fish.

There is a close link between filtration and aeration, bringing
oxygen into contact with the water. This is most obviously seen in
the case of the airlift tube that connects with the base plate of the
undergravel filter. It takes water that has passed through the filter
bed back up to the surface of the aquarium, mixing it with bubbles
of air. Yet the main function of this activity is to cause movement
of the water in the aquarium, leading to increased contact between
the atmospheric air and the water in the tank. This interaction provides the best trigger not just for reoxygenation, but also for carbon dioxide to diffuse out of the water. It is for this reason that the
outlet of a power filter needs to be located just at water level, and
not below it, in order to create movement of the water here, with
the nozzle here usually being adjustable.

Water circulation

Movement of the water in the aquarium is not just important for oxy-
genation, however. It also ensures that the temperature of the water
is relatively constant. Otherwise, the warm water can rise to the top
of the tank, while colder water is present near the base, which can be

TRICKLE FILTERS

The trickle filter is another design of filter that has become quite popular among fish keepers, but tends to be used more in specialist fish-houses than the domestic environment.

It typically consists of a series of trays with drainage holes in their bases, filled with filter wool and sand. Water from the tank is pumped up and sprayed out over the surface of the filter, and then trickles back down through the series of trays into the aquarium. This method oxygenates the water very effectively through contact with air, assisting the conversion of nitrite (NO_2) to nitrate (NO_3).

spray bar

filter wool or sand

plastic trays with drainage holes

filtered water returns to main aquarium

⬆ A basic trickle filter system. Units such as these are sited above the main tank. They are supplied by water pumped through a spray bar from a power filter. Trickle filters help oxygenate the water flowing through them and so increase bacterial activity.

➡ Small single-tray trickle filters sited above the tank can be used effectively on breeding and rearing tanks, or where it is impractical to fit a large multi-tray unit.

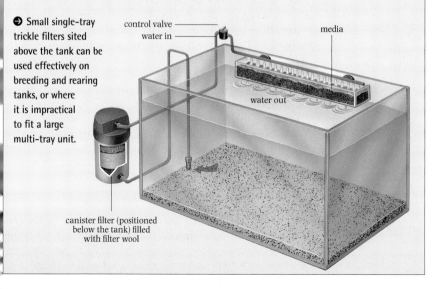

control valve

water in

media

water out

canister filter (positioned below the tank) filled with filter wool

◑ Decor can be held together where necessary with aquarium sealant. The addition of plants helps to soften the appearance. Without the planting, imagine how severe-looking this environment would be.

THE BENEFITS OF LIVING PLANTS

Plants also provide a source of additional oxygen during hours of daylight or with aquarium lighting, and help to reduce the level of dissolved carbon dioxide during this period, as part of the process of photosynthesis (*see* diagram page 19). Oxygen gas can often be seen forming streams of tiny bubbles rising from the leaves of submerged plants up through the water. When it is dark, however, this process stops, and plants then respire using oxygen rather than carbon dioxide.

particularly harmful for various catfish and similar species that inhabit the lower reaches of the tank.

Water temperature is another factor that influences the amount of dissolved oxygen present in the water. The amount of oxygen that can be absorbed into the water at a temperature of 41°F (5°C) is approximately twice as much will be present at 86°F (30°C). Although

fish from tropical waters have adapted by having correspondingly lower oxygen requirements than their coldwater counterparts, you need to ensure the oxygen level in their aquarium does not become further depleted. Good aeration is very significant in this respect. Within the tank itself, breaking up the output of bubbles via a diffuser or similar unit into a finer stream of bubbles will mean that more of the oxygen will be retained within the water.

PLANTS AND PLANTING

As part of the natural ecosystem, plants have significant roles to play in aquarium surroundings, ranging from the utilization of dissolved nitrate to providing shelter and spawning sites for the fish themselves. Hatchetfish (Gasteropelecidae), for example, will congregate under floating plants that conceal their presence, darting out to obtain insects that come within their reach here. Providing an environment of this type in the aquarium will help the fish settle down quickly and, being less stressed, they are also more likely to remain healthy. You can also enjoy observing their normal behavior at close quarters.

⬆ The aquarium needs to be carefully planned to mirror the needs of your fish, although this still leaves plenty of scope to create an individual biotope. So-called pagoda rocks have been used here to add both vertical and horizontal visual interest.

It is important to choose the right type of plants for a particular aquarium. For example, it is difficult to maintain an attractively planted goldfish tank. This is partly because there is a narrower choice of coldwater plants, compared with the wide array available for tropical aquariums. More significant, however, is the fact that goldfish are bottom-feeders, and will inevitably dig in the substrate in search of food, dislodging plants in the process. These coldwater fish may also nibble at the leaves, inhibiting the plant's growth. In this case, it may be better to leave the substrate relatively free of vegetation, while using floating plants at the surface. Digging up plants is a particular problem in the case of various large cichlids as well.

Red oranda (*Carassius auratus* var.), a fancy goldfish variety with lily.

In some cases, plants can also be vital for the survival of fish. A densely planted aquarium will be a very important retreat for the young offspring of guppies and other livebearers, to protect them from being eaten by the other fish in the tank. Unfortunately, it is not always easy to establish and grow plants successfully in aquarium surroundings. This may be the result of inadequate lighting, especially if the type of light does not correspond to the natural rays of sunlight. Even with suitable lighting however, the intensity and length of exposure may be inadequate to meet the needs of the plants, causing them to turn yellow and ultimately die back.

There can also be difficulties with the plants themselves. While there are many types of tropical plants cultivated and sold for aquariums, not all of these are suited to growing in a permanently aquatic environment. While they root below the water line, some plants will rapidly grow up through shallow water into the air, being more like marsh plants than truly aquatic. These are the least likely to thrive in a traditional aquarium, typically rotting back under these conditions.

When seeking plants for the aquarium, you can buy collections of various plants recommended for tanks of different sizes. These are sometimes available by mail, although it may be better to choose the plants yourself locally, so that they can be transferred back to water

⊕ Some of the many aquarium plants now grown by specialist suppliers. Clockwise from top left: water wisteria (*Hygrophila difformis*); ambulia (*Limnophila sessiflora*); corkscrew vallis (*Vallisneria torta*); *Ludwigia* sp.

with minimal delay. Even so, you are likely to find that there will be some dying back of the leaves until the plants have adjusted to their new environment. Alternatively, you can choose plants that you like, and build up an aquarium garden of your choice.

An excellent effect can be created by choosing a specimen plant to grow toward the back of the aquarium, where it will catch the eye. The sides are often quite densely planted, leaving a more extensive swimming area for the fish toward the front of the aquarium, where they will be more visible. Small, low-growing clusters of plants can be used here. Some aquatic plants can be trained to grow quite easily on other decor within the aquarium.

Finally, some floating plants can be cultivated on the surface of the water, but remember to keep an adequate gap here between the water level and the hood. This will prevent these plants from being concealed and from rotting as the result of condensation from the splash shield protecting the lights.

How plants are sold

The cultivation of plants for the aquarium market has become a huge worldwide industry, and there are a number of ways in which they are now offered for sale. The most basic is in the form of unrooted shoots, which can be used as cuttings. Coldwater plants such as *Elodea* (Canadian pondweed), which is a popular choice for goldfish aquariums, are often sold in this way. They are inexpensive, and the bundle simply needs to be divided up and planted. It is usually better to trim the stems so the crushed area, where the shoots were tied, is removed. This area is less likely to root successfully, and may instead just rot. Weigh the shoots down with stones or ornaments to encourage rooting and as a way of preventing the fish from digging them up easily.

You can also buy what are often described as bare-rooted plants. These are in effect cuttings that have already started to develop roots, and so in theory, should transplant more reliably. Unfortunately, those that have become damaged in transit are just as likely to die back as the bunched types. It is important to check carefully for any signs of damage, particularly at the base of the plant close to the roots. Any damage to the roots is probably less significant than crushing of the stem itself, although many of the plants sold in this way, such as *Vallisnerias*, are quite thick-stemmed in any case.

Potted plants, sold in plastic open-weave containers, are more expensive but usually easier to establish without any problems. These can simply be transferred into the aquarium with their roots being left undisturbed, although it is worth checking that they are rooted. Not all such plants are necessarily established: some may be just cuttings

⊙ Water lettuce, or Nile cabbage (*Pistia stratiotes*), is a floating plant that requires high to very high lighting conditions and tropical temperature, but is tolerant of most water conditions.

ⓘ PLANTING DEPTH

Never bury the crowns of aquatic plants in the substrate itself, as they will inevitably rot when planted in this way. In some cases, as with banana plants, some of the root system too should be exposed above the substrate. Rhizomes should be planted at an angle, with the bulk of the root hidden, rather than being completely buried. Bulbs should also be left partly exposed at the surface. Strip off the leaves of cuttings to at least two nodes up from the bottom of the stem, because these will rot if buried. Set each one in an individual hole, in groups to create good cover.

that have been pushed into a pot, which can make them a relatively expensive purchase. They are set in an inert material such as rock wool rather than soil, which would otherwise be dispersed in the aquarium. In general, unlike most terrestrial plants, those that grow in water rely on their roots primarily for anchorage, rather than for obtaining nutrients from their surroundings.

Plants that float on the water surface without any anchorage include *Lemna* (duckweed), which is useful for coldwater aquariums, or more tropical species such as Amazon frogbit (*Limnobium laevigatum*). With larger floating plants, ensure the leaves are not damaged, and that the center of the plant looks healthy, showing no signs of rotting off and dying back.

Floating plants spread quite rapidly under favorable conditions, so just a few will be needed at the outset. However, they often end up in a corner of the aquarium, because of the movement of the water. If necessary, you can reposition them above another part of the aquarium by adjusting the direction of the nozzle of an internal power filter.

Riccia fluitans is a popular and versatile floating plant for the tropical aquarium, forming a solid green mass. It is especially

⊙ Planting an *anubias* species in the substrate. Be sure of the likely size to which aquarium plants may grow, planting them as required to the appropriate depth in the substrate.

TRAINED PLANTS

You can buy plants that have been trained on to rockwork or bogwood, but by purchasing the plants loose, it should not take long to achieve the same effect. Simply use rubber bands to attach the plant to the desired base; the bands can be cut off once it has anchored itself in place. Popular plants cultivated in this way include Java fern (*Microsorum pteropus*) and Java moss (*Vesicularia dubyana*).

🔼 Riccia, or crystalwort (*Riccia fluitans*) can cover the surface in a green mass. It prefers medium-hard water conditions, but can tolerate a wide temperature range.

valuable in tanks accommodating bubble-nesters, because they can use this plant as a point of attachment for their nests. Other egg-laying fish may be attracted to spawn in this plant, however, since it grows just below the surface.

Few aquarium plants are grown from seed but especially in mild areas, you can germinate water lily seeds in a tropical aquarium, moving these plants to larger accommodation as they outgrow the aquarium itself. It is also possible to obtain rhizomes of various aquatic lilies, which should sprout into life before long. These will normally then grow well, with no risk of the leaves dying back. A typical example is the African tiger lotus (*Nymphaea maculata*), which can look stunning as a centerpiece in a large aquarium, particularly the reddish variant.

A smaller but equally attractive option is the banana plant (*Nymphoides aquatica*), whose roots resemble a clump of bananas. Its leaves extend up about 12in (30cm) through the water to the surface, and it may sometimes flower above the water line. Originating from the southern United States, the banana plant can be propagated by dividing up the rootstock or splitting off runners.

It is possible to grow a plant that prefers soft water in an environment where the water is harder, but it may not adapt as well to such surroundings, slowing its growth as a result. Those aquatic plants that are widely available are reasonably tolerant of varied growing conditions. Be aware of special needs. For example, if you are setting up a tank for Rift Valley cichlids, where the water conditions need to be hard, then it is advisable to choose the plants accordingly. Also consider lighting preferences, as some plants need a higher level of illumination to thrive. Although the African tiger lotus can be grown in hard water, it must also have high-intensity lighting.

Matching the fish to the types of plants that are found in their natural habitats is not essential, although some aquarists prefer to design what is often called a thematic tank, creating exactly the type of habitat where the fish would be found in their natural environment. Amazonian sword plants (*Echinodorus* spp.), for example, are often used in an aquarium housing small tetras and Corydoras catfish originating from this area of South America. Even so, it is impor-

ⓘ GROWING NEEDS

When choosing plants, it is not just a matter of considering how large they grow. You also need to check that their lighting needs and required water conditions will match those in the aquarium itself. A few, such as Java moss, will grow well where the surroundings are quite dark, and if kept under bright light, there is a risk that algal growth will invade the fronds, causing the plant itself to die back. Just as not all garden plants thrive in acid soils, so many aquatic plants prefer more neutral surroundings. Similarly, the hardness of the water can influence their growth, so check on these needs before finalizing your choice.

tant to bear in mind that some of these plants grow much larger than others, and to avoid those which will grow too large.

It is always a good idea to inspect the leaves of plants carefully to ensure you do not inadvertently introduce snails to the aquarium. Their eggs are often quite hard to spot, consisting in the initial stages of little more than a lump of transparent jelly with some dark dots in it. While a small number of snails will cause little harm, and add an additional focus of interest to the aquarium, they can easily build up to become a major pest, damaging the aquatic plants. This is because they are hermaphroditic, meaning each snail has both sets of sex organs present in its body, so two snails will inevitably breed, producing hundreds of eggs. These typically take about three months to hatch, with the young snails resembling miniature adults at this stage.

SNAIL DAMAGE

It is usually possible to distinguish between damage caused by snails and that resulting from fish by the shape and distribution of the plant damage. Snails have powerful mouthparts, which allow them to rasp holes in leaves, which are typically rounded in shape. Fish, in contrast, usually nibble more at the edges of plants, virtually uprooting them in some cases, and you are likely to see them doing it. It can help to add some vegetable matter to the diet, to dissuade the fish from attacking the plants. The snails as well might leave your plants alone if they scavenge on any vegetable food left by the fish.

Controlling snail numbers

Some fish eat snails, which helps to keep a check on their numbers, rather than allowing them to become rampant. Freshwater puffer-fish (*Tetraodon fluviatilis*) can crunch snail shells easily with their powerful jaws, while clown loaches (*Botia macrantha*) also eat snails readily. It is also not too difficult to trap snails in the aquarium because they like to congregate in dark places. An inverted saucer placed on the floor or the aquarium, and baited with a piece of cucumber, should allow you to catch them without difficulty.

◗ Freshwater puffer-fish. or green puffer (*Tetraodon fluviatilis*), snail-eater.

 Waterfall in
Chapada des
Guimenes, Mato
Grosso, Brazil. The
water chemistry is
influenced by the
rocks over which it
flows, and the rate of
flow too. Not many
fish are going to be
traveling upstream
from here! Geographi-
cal barriers like this
are the most obvious
reason for speciation—
the separation of
groups of living
organisms that
develop over time into
species that do not
interbreed—providing
the fantastic variety
of fish available to the
aquarist. This is not
only the home of the
Mato Grosso Acara
cichlid, but also
wholly different fish
types: the characins,
toothcarps and catfish.

Avoid using chemical means of control if you are faced with an explosion of snails. Although this treatment will kill them, their bodies will then pollute the water.

Apple snails (*Pomacea bridgesi*), originating from South America, are the most widely kept aquarium snails. A stunning bright orangish-yellow color variety is now well established in the aquarium trade, although the natural color of the shells of these mollusks is brownish. Other aquatic snails may be more suited to coldwater aquariums. Ramshorn snails (*Planorbis* spp.) have a tightly curled shell, and pond snails (*Limnaea* spp.) have a more spiral shape.

WATER CHEMISTRY

In the early days of fish keeping, the water conditions were far more critical than they are today. This was at a stage when all the fish available were caught in the wild, whereas today, the vast majority of those in trade are captive-bred, in countries as far apart as the United States and Singapore—often well away from their natural range.

One of the consequences is that the fish themselves have adapt-ed somewhat to water chemistry that is different from that found in their wild habitat, although you should aim to maintain this as closely as possible. While the fish may apparently live quite satis-factorily in conditions where the water chemistry is not optimal, they are far less likely to breed in such surroundings.

There are two important components to water chemistry, although they are linked to some extent. The first is the relative hardness of the water. Pure rainwater when it falls contains no dissolved salts, so that it is described as soft. Many aquarium fish originate from rivers that are swollen directly by rainfall, and so require soft water conditions. Rainwater running over rocks, however, can alter its character, espe-cially in areas such as the Rift Valley in Africa where it comes into contact with limestone rocks. It then picks up ions that change its chemical composition, causing it to become hard in this case. By contrast, this does not occur in areas of granite, simply because the granite is insoluble. The chemistry of rainwater falling in such regions is unaffected by contact with this stone. This is important in the context of choice of aquarium decor.

Hardness

Water hardness takes two forms, with bicarbonate salts of calcium or magnesium being responsible for temporary hardness, often abbreviated to KH. This can be removed by boiling, which precipitates the bicarbonate from the water, creating the so-called "fur" seen in kettles in hard-water areas. The other component of hardness is permanent hardness, caused by the presence of calcium and magnesium sulfate, as well as chlorates and nitrates, which cannot be altered by boiling the water. This is often described as GH, but beware because sometimes this is used as an indicator of total hardness as well.

Unfortunately, several different systems were used in the past for measuring water hardness and this has led to confusion. The tendency today is to use the international measurement of milligrams per liter (abbreviated to mg/l), which is the same as parts per million (ppm). It is possible to convert older units to mg/l simply by multiplying them as shown:

American degree × 17.1
English (or Clark) degree × 14.3
German degree (degree D) × 17.9

Hardness can vary from 50mg/l or less to a reading in excess of 300mg/l, which is regarded as very hard. A figure of approximately 100mg/l is seen as the crossover point between soft and hard water

---

① VARIATIONS IN MEASURING HARDNESS

As a rough guide to the water conditions in your area, soft water forms lather much more readily with soap compared with hard water, although a more accurate assessment will be important in aquarium surroundings. Tests kits to measure water hardness are available from aquatic outlets, but they can be measuring different degrees of hardness. Some will determine KH while others give a GH reading, so it is important to be sure that the test results are consistent. There may also be anomalies in some cases, with certain KH kits not distinguishing between the magnesium and calcium salts responsible for temporary hardness. The presence of sodium carbonate can also cause an unexpectedly high KH reading.

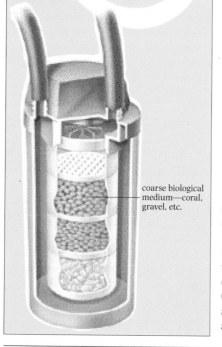

FILTRATION AND pH

It is not only the fish and plants in an aquarium that can be affected by the pH of the water. This can also affect the beneficial bacteria forming part of a biological filter. Their activity will be seriously compromised at pH levels below 6, and this in turn will affect the water quality. As a result, the fish show typical signs of a shift in pH, which can soon prove fatal. Aquariums housing fish such as tetras (which require acidic, soft water) are most vulnerable to filtration problems of this type. As an additional safeguard, you can add a sachet of zeolite to the filter. This will adsorb ammonia directly from the water, lessening the reliance on biological filtration in the aquarium.

coarse biological medium—coral, gravel, etc.

THE SIGNIFICANCE OF pH

The other important aspect of water chemistry is the relative degree of acidity, known as pH, which is derived from a logarithmic scale, ranging from 0 to 14. A pH figure of 7.2 is considered as neutral: anything below this figure counts as acidic, while above it is alkaline. The pH relates directly to the chemical structure of water, which is H_2O, consisting of a combination of hydrogen (H) and hydroxyl (HO) ions. If there are more hydrogen ions in the water than hydroxyl, then the water will be acidic, whereas a preponderance of hydroxyl ions makes it alkaline. It is quite easy to test the pH of water samples using either test kits or more sophisticated pH meters, which give a digital readout.

Fish habitats and pH

Fish are generally found in waters that have a pH reading in the range between 5 and 9.5. Just a shift from pH7 to pH8 marks a very significant alteration, because the concentration of hydroxyl ions will increase by a factor of ten. Fish live within quite tightly defined pH boundaries, although they can adapt, especially over a period of time, by shifting the bicarbonate level of their blood.

An increase in bicarbonate prevents a fall in pH, and a rise in pH will see the concentration of bicarbonate ions fall, to bring the figure back down again. The phenomenon of holding the pH steady in this way is known as buffering, with the mechanism itself being regulated both by a hormone in the blood and also the gills through which the fish obtains oxygen from the water.

Within the aquarium, the pH will naturally over a period of time tend to fall. As the fish's waste builds up in the aquarium, this causes the water to become more acidic. Gaseous changes also have an impact, such as the carbon dioxide released by the fish and aquarium plants at night, while photosynthesis raises the pH back again by utilizing this gas. The substrate can also have an influence. Limestone, for example, reacts with the water and serves to lower the pH.

Modifying water chemistry

The first step is to carry out tests on your drinking water to determine its relative degree of hardness and the pH value, which should not vary significantly over a period of time (see p.111). You then need to compare these figures with the needs of the fish that you are planning to keep. Even if they do not correspond, you should be able to adjust the water chemistry to the required level for this purpose in the aquarium, but some trial and error may be required at the outset. Consequently you should set up the tank before acquiring any fish, to ensure that the environment will be suitable for them.

It is possible to carry out adjustments to water chemistry in a number of ways. Increasing the level of hardness is quite straightforward, being achieved just by adding limestone or similar calcareous rocks to the tank. This can be in the form of boulders, as gravel or even in sachets placed within a canister filter.

The simplest way of softening water is to use freshly collected rainwater, but few fish keepers now use this method because of worries about possible pollutants in this water, and a likely accompanying acidic pH. Distilled water is a safer option and can be bought easily without the need to depend on rainfall, but it can lack other chemicals that would normally aid plant growth.

There are also other more technical choices now available for water-softening purposes, such as a special aquarium ion exchange resin. This in effect swaps the calcium ions for hydrogen, although the initial water run off the system must be discarded because there may be toxic chemicals present in it. Be sure to use a hydrogen ion exchange column, rather than a sulfur-based one, simply because this will otherwise have the undesirable effect of increasing the pH.

Making the pH in the aquarium lower is quite easily accomplished if you have a canister filter, by incorporating a sachet of special aquarium peat here. This will need replacing every three weeks or so in order to remain effective. When you want a more alkaline environment for fish, as in the case of Rift Valley cichlids, this can be simply achieved by using a limestone substrate.

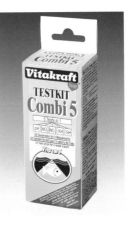

● The first time you use a water test kit should probably be on your home water supply, to pre-empt later difficulties with aquarium water quality. There are many test kits available able to indicate multiple water attributes: pH, nitrite and nitrate levels, carbonate hardness and total hardness.

⚠ pH AND AMMONIA

A build-up of ammonia from the fish's waste is especially dangerous under alkaline water conditions, because of the relative proportions of hydrogen and hydroxyl ions. In this situation, there will be far fewer hydrogen ions available to combine with the free ammonia, so that it represents more of a hazard to the fish's health.

● Air-stones being positioned and held by a handful of gravel before the rest of the gravel, rockwork and eventually water is put in.

● An undergravel filter plate in place, partly covered by gravel. The airlift is fitted with a diffuser stone. As a rough rule-of-thumb, for an undergravel filter to work you should cover it with at least 3in (8 cm) of gravel at the front of the tank, rising to as much as double that at the back.

ASSEMBLY

It is not normally a good idea to buy the fish at the same time as the aquarium, even if you are buying one of the modern complete acrylic designs with all the components in place (apart from the substrate) that simply need to be filled with water. If there is any fault in the system, you could be stranded with fish when you cannot maintain the correct environmental conditions for them. It also helps to allow perhaps a week for the system to settle down, once it is operating, particularly if you are including living plants.

Once the undergravel filter plate (which must extend over the entire base of the aquarium) is in place, you can add a so-called "gravel tidy," which helps to prevent the slits in the plate from becoming blocked by substrate. You can then tip the washed gravel on top. It needs to extend to a minimum depth of at least 3in (8cm) over the entire area, although it helps to incorporate a slight slope, extending from the back of the tank down to the front. This will allow you to spot and remove debris that may be too large for the filter.

Having mapped out a planting plan, set the plants in place accordingly. It is very important to ensure that the leaves do not become desiccated, because they will inevitably die back soon afterward. In the case of those plants that are in pots, dig a hole in

the gravel and bury the pot as far as possible. You may ultimately need to scoop up the gravel around the base to disguise the presence of the pot in due course; alternatively, it may be possible to conceal it with aquarium decor such as rockwork. Especially with an undergravel filter, it is better to keep the plants in pots, simply because otherwise their roots may spread and block off the holes in the filter and compromise its efficiency.

It is recommended to pour some water into the aquarium first, as this makes it less likely that the plants will be disturbed by the swirling water when the tank is ultimately filled. You can minimize the disturbance to the gravel bed by pouring the water at first on to a saucer placed on top of the gravel.

It is also easier to carry out the rest of the landscaping in the tank before it has been filled completely. The heaterstat should be sited either at one end or preferably at the back of the tank, being set horizontally here, but raised above the substrate and not surrounded by decor. In particular, ensure plants do not come into contact with the heater, as this will burn their leaves, while blocking off the flow of

↑ A brackish (part-salt) aquarium set-up with plastic plants and natural rocks. Be certain that all rocks included will not have adverse effects on the water chemistry. Covering the floor area in this way with rocks can compromise the activity of an undergravel filter.

➊ It can be useful to make a plan of the layout of lava rock before putting it into the aquarium. In fact, such prior planning on paper is sensible for your entire planting and rockwork scheme. Lava rock can be quite easily broken up with a hammer to create the desired effect.

water with decor will prevent the water being heated evenly.

Wood and rockwork can be incorporated into the aquarium, not only to create a natural setting but also to divide the tank so that there are plenty of retreats for the occupants. This will help to prevent nervous individuals from disturbing the other members of a community aquarium; it also lessens the likelihood of any bullying, which can ultimately prove fatal. Recent studies have also confirmed that some catfish benefit from having wood that they can rasp in their diet.

Bogwood sold for aquariums is a natural product and comes in a range of shapes and sizes. It generally needs to be soaked for a period before being placed in the aquarium, because otherwise it is likely to turn the water yellow thanks to the tannins that it contains, although you may be offered varnished bogwood which is effectively sealed. There may be a risk that the fish could poison themselves if they nibble at this coating, and species from the Amazonian region may actually benefit from being kept in tannic water. In other cases, artificial wood may be the best option. Always position wood so that it is well bedded in the substrate, to prevent its floating up to the surface once the tank is filled. It is also possible to create extra interest by fixing plants such as Java moss to either real or artificial wood in the aquarium, helping to soften its outlines.

ROCKWORK

Rockwork is useful, not just as decor but also as potential spawning sites for fish such as discus (*Symphysodon discus*), which may otherwise be drawn to lay their eggs with fatal consequences on the aquarium heater. You can buy suitable rocks from aquatic stores; they are usually sold by weight. It is, of course, important to avoid any calciferous rocks, unless you are seeking to modify the water chemistry. Granite is popular, appearing more colorful when wet. Slate is also widely used in aquariums, especially for spawning purposes.

Ensure that all rocks are adequately supported in the tank, so there will be no risk of their becoming dislodged. A toppling rock could seriously injure the fish or even crack the side of the tank or the heater itself. This really can happen! You can now buy lightweight hollow alternatives to rockwork, molded to look like the real thing.

When filling the tank, you need to know the volume, so you can add the correct quantity of water conditioner. Since products of this type usually state figures in both liters and gallons, it is much easier to work in liters. You simply need to multiply the height, length, and width of the aquarium in centimeters, and then divide by 1,000, to give the volume in liters. A gallon equals 3.78 liters.

A water conditioner will be essential to neutralize chemicals, both at the outset and also subsequently when undertaking partial water changes. Check if it will neutralize both chlorine and chloramine. There are test kits available to check on the levels in water, to ensure that these chemicals have been properly neutralized before you add the water to the aquarium. Fish housed in relatively acidic water run a higher risk of being affected by hypochlorous acid.

Water conditioners, as distinct from dechlorinating products, may also include other ingredients that should help fish to settle in new surroundings. Aloe vera, for example, is believed to prevent fungal infections that may follow minor skin damage.

Another useful product that should be added to a newly established aquarium is a culture of bacteria to seed the filter bed and assist with biological filtration. Introducing them in a concentrated form helps to ensure that the development of the filter bed is speeded up, lessening the risk of any ammonia build-up in the early weeks following the setting up of a new aquarium.

BACKGROUND

You may also want to add a background to the tank. There are now very effective photographic freshwater backdrops for both coldwater and tropical aquariums. These can be simply stuck on the back of the tank, being sold off a roll to suit tanks of different lengths. A backdrop will help to conceal bright wallpaper, for example, which may otherwise detract from the finished appearance of the tank, once all the components are in place.

⊙ There are both plain and more decorative backgrounds available for aquaria. You might decide against having any background if your walls are plain, as in this "species" aquarium, with male guppies and natural plants.

⚠ ELECTRICITY AND WATER

Never plug in and switch on the heater or other electrical equipment while you are still placing your hands in the water, fitting out the aquarium. There is a risk that you could receive an electrical shock, should there be any fault in the system. Similarly, do not handle plugs with wet hands, because this also dramatically increases the risk of an electrical shock. Always fit a nonreturn valve into the airline so as to prevent water being sucked into the air pump, which has to be located outside the aquarium, ideally at a higher level than the tank.

CHAPTER 3

Introducing the
Categories of Fish

Fish are categorized in different ways in terms of the home aquarium, and the breakdown often bears no relationship to the scientific classification. Divisions may be based on the water temperature that fish require, with recognized coldwater and tropical groupings, or on the basis of water chemistry needs.

Such a classification helps to reinforce the fact that fish preferring hard water, such as the various cichlids from the lakes of East Africa, cannot be mixed with fish from soft-water areas such as the Amazon. Then there are their dietary preferences, since clearly some fish are carnivorous in their feeding habits and so compatibility becomes a major issue in terms of their housing. Choosing compatible tankmates therefore requires care, particularly as guidelines on the temperament of the fish themselves are not infallible.

THE VARIOUS GROUPS: HOW TAXONOMY WORKS

The divisions in the following section are based on the scientific groupings to which the fish belong. Shared physical characteristics, however, do not imply shared aquarium needs. You cannot simply assume that the needs of all the fish in a group are the same simply because they are classified together taxonomically. This is particularly important when setting up a community aquarium— you need to discover more about the actual habits of the individual fish. Those covered in this chapter reflect those species that are widely available, and, in many cases, will be suitable for a community aquarium, as well as a few with more specialist needs.

Classification tools

The way in which fish are named is a branch of the science known as taxonomy. Taxonomy works through a series of so-called ranks,

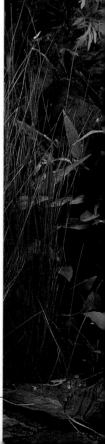

being part of a universal system applied to all living organisms, as well as fossils. Although scientific names may appear of little use to fish-keepers, they can be helpful since they can indicate the appearance of a fish.

A scientific name is unique, whereas two or more different types of fish can share a common name, leading to possible confusion. Scientific names are also international, irrespective of the language spoken. It is also possible to distinguish between closely related forms of the same fish; this is usually not feasible when you are relying on a common name.

As an example of how the system works, all life forms belong to the animal kingdom, with fish forming a distinctive class, along with mammals, birds, and other similar broad groupings. Below this, fish are subdivided into various orders, such as the Perciformes. These orders are in turn split into families, such as the Anabantidae and Cichlidae in this particular case.

⬇ A community aquarium using rustic slate and natural plant decor. The same classificatory system applies to aquarium plants as well as fish.

Each family of fish is made up of a number of genera (singular "genus"); the Anabantidae family, for example, includes the genera *Betta*, *Trichogaster*, and *Macropodus*. This level in the taxonomic tree is an important grouping as far as aquarists are concerned, because it reveals which fish are quite closely related. Each genus consists of various species, which can be recognized because their name is made up of two parts, such as *Betta splendens*, in the case of the popular Siamese fighting fish. The genus and species name should always be in italics.

There is one further level below that of the species, which separates very closely related forms into subspecies (usually abbreviated to "ssp."). The blind cave fish, for example, is classified as a distinctive subspecies, *Astyanax fasciatus mexicanus*, separating it from the so-called nominate race, *Astyanax fasciatus fasciatus*. The nominate race is always the one that was recognized first, as indicated by the repetition of the scientific name—in some cases, however, it may not even be the most common. There are strict rules governing the naming of all organisms. In order to be given a scientific name, there must be a specimen collected and described, being lodged in a museum or similar scientific collection. This is known as the type specimen.

⊙ Blind cave fish,
Astyanax fasciatus mexicanus ssp..

Although it may seem that we have discovered everything about the world, there are still relatively large numbers of new fish—certainly compared with other vertebrates—that are still being discovered each year. Remote areas of South America and Borneo are two areas that hold great promise for ichthyologists in search of new species of fish. It is remarkable to reflect that some of those most commonly kept in aquariums today are actually quite recent discoveries in scientific terms. This is partly because many fish may have quite limited distributions. The stunning neon tetra (*Paracheirodon innesi*), for example, only became known in 1936, after being discovered in the Rio Putumayo in eastern Peru.

Even in the wild, the brilliance of the cardinal tetras shines through the opaque, tannic water. Photographed in the Rio Negro, in northern Brazil, their tight-knit maneuvers are a reminder that cardinals are best kept as a group (see page 63).

AN AQUARIST CLASSIFICATION

As studies about fish advance, and new species are discovered, so too there is often a tendency to reclassify them, usually into different genera, perhaps establishing a new genus to accommodate what were previously two distinct groupings. This can cause confusion. As a result, the so-called "L-number system" was set up as an identification tool, arising from the aquarium hobby rather than from taxonomists. It arose from a realization that changes in scientific nomenclature were often confusing, particularly when new names were being adopted alongside those that had been in longstanding usage.

It was therefore decided that each known species would be provided with a unique seven-figure number, which would not change, irrespective of the scientific name. This has become known as the L-number system, because it was first applied to catfish forming the Loricariidae family, although other groups of fish have different letters associated with them. South American cichlids, for example, begin with the identity letter S. Linked to a photographic database, this system also allows distinctive local fish populations to be identified. The L-number system has now become widely used by those in the trade, since being devised in the early 1990s, and specialist retailers often advertise stock on this basis.

Any color variants that have cropped up as the result of captive breeding are not ascribed new scientific names. They remain listed under the species name, but may have the letters "var" (indicating a variant or variety) appended at the end of their name, followed by that of the variety concerned.

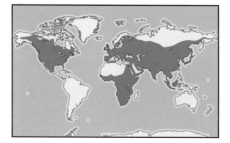

◐ Cyprinid
distribution.

CYPRINIDS

This grouping includes the world's most popular aquarium fish, the goldfish (*Carassius auratus*), as well as many widely kept members of community aquariums. Most of these fish are small and ideally suited to this type of environment, but there are a few exceptions, such as the tinfoil barb (*Barbus schwanenfeldi*), which will rapidly outgrow its companions, reaching a length of 12in (30cm) or more, and requiring correspondingly larger accommodation.

Goldfish

The goldfish (*Carassius auratus*) has a history of domestication which stretches back over 1,000 years in its native China. Its ancestors were dull grayish-green carp living in slow-flowing waterways, and often caught for food. Once color variants started to emerge, some were taken to Japan in the 1500s, and then from here, goldfish were introduced to Europe about 200 years later. Their adaptability ensured their popularity at this stage, long before it was possible to keep tropical fish successfully in temperate areas.

Today, there are probably more than 150 different documented varieties of goldfish; new ones, such as the so-called panda (because of its predominantly black and white coloration) are still being developed. If you are interested in exhibiting fish, goldfish are a good choice, especially as there are well-established judging standards laid down for all the popular varieties.

Certain types, such as the sleek and active comet, are better suited to being kept in a pond, and can generally be kept outside throughout the year. In contrast however, the graceful, flowing fins of varieties such as the veiltail can only be fully appreciated in an aquarium; furthermore, these fish are not hardy in temperate areas. Although it is possible to keep them in a pond over the summer, a significant drop in water temperature is likely to lead to fin rot. Always check the fins of these goldfish and similar varieties as they are often prone to this problem if the water quality is not ideal.

One of the most distinctive varieties of goldfish is the lionhead, so called because of the manelike swellings that become evident on the head of these fish as they mature. The development of this so-called hood can be a slow process, taking place over several years. Orandas are closely related to lionheads, but easily distinguished by having a dorsal fin on the top of the body, which is absent in lionheads.

Another highly distinctive form of goldfish is the pearlscale, so called because of its whitish raised scales, which create an impression

⭐ GOLDFISH

Carassius auratus
Distribution: China
Length: Typically up to 12in (30cm); often smaller
Temperament: Not aggressive
Food: Omnivorous

Blood-red goldfish.

Butterfly panda.

Long-tailed shubunkin.

Red bubble-eye.

Pearlscale oranda.

of pearls running down the sides of the body. These fish were first bred in China, originating in Kwangtung province, and are now commonly available in the West. They are another so-called fancy variety, with a corpulent body and so better suited to the home aquarium.

Goldfish are now bred in a wide range of colors: yellow through orange to silvery shades and the blue hues, which are a feature of the hardy shubunkins. But perhaps the most distinctive, in terms of its coloration, is the moor. It can be recognized by its matt black appearance, sometimes turning a deep shade of bronze on the underside of the body. Their eyes, described as telescope-eyed in cases where these are protuberant, distinguish different types of the moor. The arrangement of their fins can also differ; creating butterfly moors as an example. Similar variations in appearance are also common in other fancy goldfish.

There are other varieties of fancy goldfish characterized on the basis of their eyes alone, with this feature needing to be taken into account in their housing. The bubble-eye has distinctive jelly filled sacs under its eyes. These are quite vulnerable to injury, and so these goldfish should be housed in fairly bare aquariums, with no rockwork.

○ Blue butterfly moor. Note the enlarged eyes, a feature of these particularly fancy goldfish.

The celestial gets its name because of the way in which its eyes are directed horizontally, rather than being located vertically on the sides of the head as usual. Celestials can be at a disadvantage in the company of other goldfish, especially when seeking food, so are often kept on their own. They also need a clear area for swimming, rather than a heavily decorated aquarium.

Goldfish still display a number of the attributes of their wild ancestors, including rooting about on the floor of their aquarium in search of food. This means that it can be very difficult to establish plants successfully in a goldfish tank, especially as the fish may browse on the leaves and shoots. The choice is also more limited, because the water is unheated, but Canadian pondweed (*Elodea densa*) is a good choice. A powerful filtration system is necessary in goldfish aquariums as well, particularly for larger fish, along with good aeration. There are a number of special goldfish diets on the market.

Male fish develop white spots on their gill plates and adjacent fins at the onset of the breeding period, while females swell with eggs. Spawning can be achieved in an aquarium, but the eggs are unlikely to survive for long in a tank with the adult fish. Hatching usually takes place after about four days, depending on the water temperature. All young goldfish display the dark appearance of their ancestors at first, and it takes from two months to a year for their adult coloration to start to emerge, usually along their underparts. In any spawning, however, there may be a few fish that never change color.

White cloud mountain minnow

China is also the home of the white cloud mountain minnow (*Tanichthys albonubes*), another cyprinid that can be kept in an unheated aquarium. It comes from the mountainous region close to Canton. These fish are very easy to cater for, and will show to best effect in a shoal. Breeding in aquarium surroundings is quite possible, with females recognizable by their smaller size and the redder coloration around the mouth. Raising the water temperature slightly to about 72°F (22°C) can trigger spawning activity. Their eggs are scattered in fine-leaved plants such as *Myriophyllum*, and they should start to hatch within two days. There is now a color variant of this species, known as the red-finned, which is recognizable by the red edges to the dorsal and anal fins, as well as a distinctive long-finned form.

★ WHITE CLOUD MOUNTAIN MINNOW

Tanichthys albonubes
Distribution: China
Length: 1.75in (4.5cm)
Temperament: Social, not aggressive
Food: Omnivorous
Water temperature: Can be as low as 50°F (15°C) in winter, 64-77°F (18-25°C) at other times

Tiger barb

The description of barb comes from the whisker-like barbels, present in many species close to the mouth, which help to provide these fish with sensory information about their environment. These fish usually inhabit the middle level area downward to the floor of the aquarium. The tiger barb (*Barbus tetrazona*) is one of the most popular members of this group, and can be identified by the presence of three vertical bands around its body. It is also known as the Sumatra barb because it is found on this Indonesian island.

Well-oxygenated water conditions are very important for these fish. They will otherwise come up to the surface, gulping air while hanging almost vertically in the water. Tiger barbs need to be kept in groups of five or six individuals, with their aquarium being well planted around the sides and more open at the front. This gives the fish an opportunity to retreat if they feel threatened, while allowing them plenty of swimming space. Pairs will breed, provided water conditions are soft and slightly acidic. They scatter their eggs, with hatching occurring within a couple of days. Various color variants and a long-finned form have been developed as a result of domestication. A very similar species, sometimes confused with the tiger barb, is the five-banded barb (*B. pentazona*). It can be distinguished by the presence of five rather than three black bands encircling its body.

⭐ TIGER BARB

Barbus tetrazona
Distribution: Sumatra
Length: 3in (7.5cm)
Temperament: Can harass long-finned fish
Food: Omnivorous
Water temperature: 68-79°F (20-26°C)

Tiger barbs may tend to nip the fins of some tank companions.

Cherry barb

The cherry barb (*Barbus titteya*) is another Asiatic species, originating from the southwest of Sri Lanka. It is quite peaceful by nature, and less inclined to engage in fin nipping, compared with tiger barbs. Care is similar, although it is slightly shyer and less active, so that you should probably add more cover in its quarters. Diffused lighting in the aquarium, created by floating plants, will also help to overcome their instinctive nervousness.

There is some natural variation in the color of cherry barbs, but only male fish display the bright cherry-red coloration, with females being much browner in appearance. A slight increase in the water temperature may encourage spawning behavior, but as with all barbs, unless the water chemistry is correct, breeding is most unlikely to occur.

⭐ CHERRY BARB

Barbus titteya
Distribution: Sri Lanka
Length: 2in (5cm)
Temperament: Social
Food: Omnivorous
Water temperature: 72-75°F (22-24°C)

Rosy barb

Even more colorful is the rosy barb (*Barbus conchonius*), with this distinctive reddish coloration being most evident in the case of male fish in breeding condition. Originating from parts of northern India, these barbs can be kept at relatively cool temperatures, down to 64°F (18°C), although they are more commonly accommodated in a typical tropical aquarium setup. It is better to acquire a small shoal of rosy barbs since this species is social by nature. Sexing is generally straightforward, especially since the fins of females are lacking in color, whereas those of males are distinctly pinkish, even outside the breeding period.

★ ROSY BARB

Barbus conchonius
Distribution: Northern India
Length: 4in (10cm)
Temperament: Social
Food: Eats prepared and live foods
Water temperature: 64-77°F (18-25°C)

This species can be recommended as one of the easiest barbs to spawn successfully in aquarium surroundings. A separate spawning tank is required to save the eggs from being eaten.

Zebra danio

Danios often have attractive patterning on their bodies, and the zebra danio is no exception. It is so called because of the horizontal stripes running down the sides of its body, although the overall markings of these fish differ somewhat, between individuals. Male fish can be recognized quite easily during the spawning period, when they are at their most colorful, as well as being slimmer than females. Interestingly, members of a pair appear to develop quite a strong pair bond, so try to identify them by their patterning, as this will enable you to transfer the correct fish across to the spawning tank. There are several variants now established, including the so-called leopard danio, which until recently used to be considered as a separate species, with more spotted patterning. There is also an attractive golden-yellow variety, and long-finned forms.

⭐ ZEBRA DANIO

Brachydanio rerio
Distribution: Eastern India
Length: 1.75in (4.5cm)
Temperament: Highly social
Food: Eats flake and small live foods
Water temperature: 64–75°F (18–24°C)

Red rasbora

The common name of these fish derives from their former generic name, which was Rasbora. Also known as the harlequin, this particular species can be easily distinguished from related rasboras by the large size of the black cones on its flanks, which extend down toward the tail, narrowing to a point, surrounded by reddish borders. It is usually possible to distinguish the sexes, particularly when there are a group of these fish. The underside of the body is more curved in the case of females, creating the impression of a wider body. Males appear thinner, and are often more brightly colored displaying a stronger red hue. Soft, acidic water conditions are required by these fish, to induce successful spawning. Females lay their eggs on broad leafed-plants such as cryptocorynes, and after spawning has occurred, the fish should be transferred back to the main aquarium, because otherwise, they are likely to consume them. Red rasboras are ideal occupants for a community tank, although they do prefer fairly subdued lighting, which can be created by the inclusion of floating plants at the water surface.

⭐ RED RASBORA

Trigonostigma heteromorpha
Distribution: Malay peninsula, Sumatra
Length: 1.75in (4.5cm)
Temperament: Social and nonaggressive
Food: Prepared foods
Water temperature: 73–79°F (22–26°C)

Some red rasboras display less silver coloration than others.

Red-tailed black shark

In spite of its name, this fish is a true cyprinid, even possessing distinctive short barbels on each side of its mouth. Its popular name is derived from its appearance, as it has a relatively high dorsal fin, and a torpedo-like body. The coloration of these fish will only be seen at its best if water conditions are favorable. Otherwise, its body color will appear as dark gray, rather than an appealing mat black, with the red coloration of the tail also being paler than normal.

Even though you may see small examples of this species being kept together on dealers' premises, the red-tailed black shark is emphatically not a social species, as far as others of its kind are concerned, although individual specimens will thrive without being aggressive in the company of unrelated fish. Even housing the red-tailed in the company of a red-finned shark (*E. frenatus*) is liable to lead to serious conflict.

Perhaps not surprisingly therefore, very little has been documented about the breeding of this species in aquariums, although it has been recorded that females spawn in a depression in the substrate. It is only just before this point that the sexes can be told apart, when the female swells with eggs. The young are silvery-brown at first, only developing their characteristic red tail when they reach seven weeks old. Red-tailed black sharks are instinctively quite shy by nature. They occupy the lower reaches of the aquarium, and should be provided with suitable cover here, in the guise of rocks and bogwood.

⭐ **RED-TAILED BLACK SHARK**

Epalzeorhynchus bicolor
Distribution: Thailand
Length: 6in (15cm)
Temperament: Not social with its own kind
Food: Pellets and some greenstuff
Water temperature: 73-79°F (22-26°C)

Unlike many other cyprinids, these fish will not live peacably with their own species.

CHARACINS

There are approximately 1,350 species of characoids, whose distribution is centered largely on the Americas, although just over 200 representatives of the order Characiformes are present in Africa. One of the most obvious distinguished features of these fish is the presence

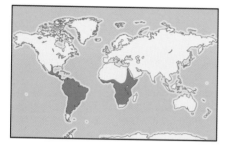

Characin distribution.

of a small adipose fin, positioned on the back between the dorsal and caudal fins. Less obvious is their very sensitive hearing. This results from a bony connection linking the swim bladder to the inner ear.

Although the most popular group with the large Characidae family as far as fishkeepers are concerned is the tetras, other members of the family that are seen occasionally include the notorious piranhas (*Serrasalmus* sp.). Another feature of these fish is that all of them, including the smallest members of the group, have well-developed teeth.

Neon tetra

The neon, so-called because the brilliance of its color matches that of a display sign, is one of the most widely kept tropical fish in the world, bred commercially in huge numbers. It is important to buy a group of neons together, as they form tightly knit shoals, and will show to best effect in this way. Males can usually be recognized as the bluish line running down the sides of their bodies is thinner and straighter than that of females. Beware of purchasing any of these fish displaying very pale coloration however, as this can be indicative of the illness known as neon tetra disease (*see* page 136).

Soft, acidic water is necessary for these fish, and under these conditions, spawning can be accomplished without too much difficulty. Females swell with eggs at this stage, and will be pursued by males. The female then adopts a near vertical position in the water immediately before releasing her eggs. There are a number of color variants of the neon tetra that have been evolved, but generally, they are not as striking in this instance as the natural form. Neons can be surprisingly long-lived fish, in spite of their small size, with individuals having been recorded as living for more than ten years in aquarium surroundings.

⭐ NEON TETRA

Paracheirodon innesi
Distribution: Rio Putumayo, eastern Peru
Length: 1.5in (3.75cm)
Temperament: Social, not aggressive
Food: Flake, live foods
Water temperature: 73-81°F (23-27°C)

Cardinal tetra

Similar in appearance but even more colorful than the neon (*P. innesi*), the cardinal can be easily distinguished by the red stripe which extends right along the sides of its body, rather than just being confined to the rear half. Its requirements are similar, however, and the addition of aquarium peat to the filtration system will help to create the tannic conditions in which these fish naturally live in the wild. A well-planted tank and subdued lighting will replicate the conditions favored by these tetras in the wild.

Their care presents no particular problems, and the likelihood of successful spawning will be enhanced by the addition of live food such as whiteworm to their diet. They are not the easiest of the tetras to breed however, with the water conditions being particularly critical. Females scatter their eggs through vegetation. Hatching takes place after about a day and then it will be a further five days before the fry are free-swimming.

★ CARDINAL TETRA

Paracheirodon axelrodi
Distribution: Western Colombia to the Orinoco in Venezuela and tributaries of the Rio Negro in northern Brazil
Length: 2in (5cm)
Temperament: Live in shoals
Food: Flake and live food
Water temperature: 73-81°F (23-27°C)

Head-and-tail light tetra

The most widely available form of this tetra, from the lower reaches of the Amazon, has a distinctive reddish area above the eyes, and two similar orange-red areas on both the upper and lower parts of the tail fin, which is why it is known as the head-and-tail light tetra. It also has a clearly defined black spot with a golden border behind each of the gill covers, so that it is more colorful overall than the other subspecies, which is found in the Amazon basin.

Sexing is not easy outside the breeding period, but males then often develop a white spot on the anal fin, while female fish swell with eggs. They may produce as many as 300 at a single spawning, usually laying in the first part of the day. Hatching takes place within 48 hours, and the young should have grown sufficiently to be offered brine shrimp nauplii by the time they are a week old. Prior to this, as with other tetras, they require a proprietary fry food, of the type produced for egg-laying fish.

Black neon

In spite of its common name, this particular fish should not be confused with the widely kept and more colorful neon (*see* page 62), especially as they are not closely related. The black neon belongs to a different genus, and occurs much further south. The feature which they do have in common is iridescent greenish coloration running down the sides of the body, although this can be more yellowish than green in the case of the black neon. Black neons require soft, acidic water and relatively dark surroundings, with floating plants in the aquarium helping to diffuse the lighting above. Otherwise, the black stripe extending down the sides of the body will appear paler under conditions of high light intensity, and also when water conditions are less than ideal.

Female black neons may be distinguished by their broader bodies, with the difference between the sexes becoming most apparent just prior to spawning, when the female swells with eggs. These tetras should be kept in a small group in the aquarium, which ought to guarantee that you have at least one pair. Good feeding, including small live food, and the use of a blackwater extract can help to trigger breeding behavior, once the fish are settled in their surroundings.

Bleeding heart tetra

There is no mistaking the unique appearance of these fish, which can be instantly recognized by the red spot, said to resemble the shape of a heart, on each side of their bodies. There are also red markings visible directly above the eyes. Sexing is also straightforward in this case since the male bleeding heart tetra has a much longer dorsal fin, as well as an enlarged anal fin. Unfortunately, however, these fish rank among the more costly tetras, and are often not suitable for a relatively small tank, because they grow to a larger size than many similar species. They are also potentially harder to establish in the confines of a new aquarium, being more prone to fungus, with males being particularly vulnerable on their fins. The use of a prepared food containing vitamin C, plus a water temperature at the higher end of the range will help to safeguard against this problem. Once the fish are well established, feeding wingless fruit flies can be valuable as a conditioner to encourage spawning, while separating the sexes for a period before reintroducing them for this purpose can also be useful.

★ BLEEDING HEART TETRA

Hyphessobrycon erythrostigma
Distribution: Upper Amazon basin
Length: Up to 4.75in (12cm)
Temperament: Male fish may sometimes squabble
Food: Prepared foods like flake and live food
Water temperature: 75-82°F (23-28°C)

A separate species with more rounded fins, *H. socolofi* from the Rio Negro, has been identified.

Lemon tetra

The coloration of these fish can be a stunning shade of lemon, although some are more silvery than others, and only if the fish are settled and water conditions ideal will their natural beauty be clearly apparent. Mature males are always a richer shade of yellow than females, and can also be distinguished by the more convex shape of the anal fins compared to females. Unfortunately, lemon tetras do not spawn as readily as some species in aquariums, although separating the sexes and conditioning them with live food can be beneficial. The female should be transferred to the spawning tank where water conditions are suitably soft and acidic, with spawning mops often being useful to encourage egg-laying. Tannic surroundings are important.

Avoid housing lemon tetras in a community aquarium in the company of young angelfish (*Pterophyllum* spp.) or other fish with elaborate fins, because they may engage in fin-nipping, often more frequently than other members of the group.

⊛ LEMON TETRA

Hyphessobrycon pulchripinnis
Distribution: Central and eastern Brazil
Length: 2in (5cm)
Temperament: Social but may fin-nip
Food: Prepared foods and small live foods
Water temperature: 73-82°F (23-28°C)

The desired yelllow coloration only appears when the fish in top condition.

Black skirt tetra

The appearance of the black skirt tetra alters noticeably as these fish grow older, with their distinctive black markings turning grayish by the time the fish are about a year old. Although the black skirt is not the most colorful of the tetras, it is one of the easiest to spawn in aquarium surroundings. The male has a more pointed dorsal fin, combined with a broader edge to the anal fin.

Originating further south from the equator than many tetras, this species is hardier, but any change in water temperature should still be performed gradually. It requires soft, acidic conditions. Live food serves as a good conditioner, and the fish should be transferred back to the main aquarium after spawning to safeguard the eggs, which will otherwise be eaten. Hatching typically occurs within 24 hours.

⊛ BLACK SKIRT TETRA

Gymnocorymbus ternetzi
Distribution: Paraguay, Bolivia, and southern Brazil
Length: 2.25in (5.5cm)
Temperament: Nonaggressive shoaler
Food: Prepared foods and small live foods
Water temperature: 68-82°F (20-28°C)

Subdued coloration is a feature of this tetra.

Congo tetra

Although the vast majority of tetras kept in aquariums originate from South America, a few African species are sometimes seen. The best known of these is probably the Congo tetra, which is characterized by its remarkable iridescence, reflecting virtually all the colors of the rainbow, from shades of yellow through red and green to blue and even tones of violet. The actual coloration depends on the individual fish, with males in general being more brightly colored than females, as well as the water quality and the lighting in the tank. Males can also be identified by their more elaborate fins and are at greatest risk from fungus as a result, especially if the water quality is poor.

Congo tetras require similar soft, acidic water conditions to their South American relatives. They can be slightly shy, especially when food is offered, and so in a community tank it is important to ensure that they are receiving sufficient to eat. Increasing the aquarium lighting may trigger breeding behavior. A spawning tank with fine-leafed plants like *Myriophyllum* should encourage the female to lay up to 300 eggs.

The adult fish must then be moved back to the main aquarium, because otherwise, they will eat the eggs. Hatching is a relatively slow process, likely to take at least five days, although unusually, the young are free-swimming from this point onward, rather than remaining quiescent in the tank for a few days. Like adult fish, they will be vulnerable to fungus, and so the presence of aquarium peat in the water is recommended as a protective measure.

★ CONGO TETRA

Micralestes interruptus
Distribution: Upper stretches of the River Congo
Length: 3in (7.5cm)
Temperament: Social, may spawn communally
Food: Flake, live foods and may even nibble greenstuff
Water temperature: 75–81°F (24–27°C)

Sexing these African tetras is very straightforward. A male fish is shown here. Those elaborate fins can regrow if damaged, provided they do not become infected.

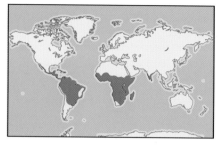

⬆ Cichlid
distribution.

CICHLIDS

This large group of about 2,000 species is widely distributed, occurring in the Americas as far north as the southern United States, and also in parts of Asia and Africa. Cichlids differ widely in their body shape and size, but there are a number of highly distinctive physical features that set them apart. They include the presence of just one not two nostril on each side of the head, and a lateral line that changes course along the length of the body. The shorter rear section is positioned at a lower level than the front area. The dorsal fin forms two distinct halves as well, with only the rear portion being flexible, while the front part is fixed.

Unfortunately, many cichlids are not suitable for a community aquarium, often because they grow too large, are too aggressive or simply because their requirements in terms of water chemistry are not compatible with most other species. This does not mean that they are difficult to keep, and it is possible in some cases to house a mixed group of these fish together. In other cases, however, they are simply too territorial, and it can be difficult to keep a pair of adult fish together because of their aggressive nature. Nevertheless, cichlids are fish with distinct personalities, and certain species can establish a strong bond with their owners, even to the extent of feeding readily from the hand.

⬇ The south-western shore of Lake Malawi. Cichlids from Lake Malawi are the most popular in the aquarium trade because they are the most colorful.

Oscar

Young oscars may appear cute when seen as a group, but it is important to appreciate they will grow rapidly and require spacious accommodation. They are not suitable companions for smaller fish, which are likely to be eaten, although it may be possible to house them satisfactorily with nonaggressive species such as large, non-predatory catfish.

Oscars can be bred quite easily in aquariums. The best way to start is to acquire a small group at the outset and allow them to pair off before they are mature. It can be very much harder to persuade an oscar to accept another companion, even of the opposite sex, once they are fully grown. Once a pair bond has formed, it lasts for life. There must be plenty of swimming space in their aquarium,

along with robust plants. Slate or bogwood should be provided as decor. Either may be chosen as a potential spawning site.

A sign that spawning is imminent is the way that both members of the pair will clean a suitable area, where the female may lay as many as 1,000 eggs. These will be guarded by the fish, as will the fry when they hatch, but soon afterward, you will need to transfer at least some of the young fish elsewhere, so they can be reared without becoming overcrowded. Spawning may take place several times in a year.

The wild form of the oscar is sometimes known as the peacock eye, because of the appearance of the distinctive marking located close to the tail base. Individuals differ in the extent and depth of their reddish coloration, one of the most colorful forms being the so-called red pearl. There is also a whitish form with variable red markings, sometimes misleadingly called an albino, as well as a long-finned variety.

★ OSCAR

Astronotus ocellatus
Distribution: Amazon, Orinoco, and Paraguay river basins
Length: As much as 13.25in (35cm)
Temperament: Territorial
Food: Prepared foods and larger live foods
Water temperature: 68-77°F (20-25°C)

A young oscar. These are fish with real personality and can become very tame.

Angelfish

The highly distinctive tall, narrow shape of these fish is no accident, because they live in areas of dense vegetation. They are therefore able to weave their way between plants with ease, which can enable them to escape from potential predators, slipping away unnoticed. Although often sold for inclusion in a community aquarium when young, angelfish will rapidly outgrow such quarters, and need a relatively deep tank, which is well planted with vegetation.

Unfortunately, sexing these cichlids is difficult outside the breeding season, although their behavior can be a helpful sign prior to egg-laying. A pair will stay close together, choosing their spawning site. Some pairs prefer to spawn on upright vegetation, such as an Amazon swordplant (*Echinodorus* sp.), whereas others may prefer to use a piece of slate for this purpose. The female will swell noticeably with her eggs at this stage, temporarily losing her characteristic slim shape.

The adult fish will remain in the vicinity of their eggs, watching over them, attempting to drive away other fish that may come too close. In due course, they oversee the hatching process and then once the fry are free-swimming, the young fish will be chaperoned to a pit excavated in the substrate of the aquarium. Their parents produce a body secretion that their offspring feed on in these early stages. Even once the young angelfish start swimming freely, the adults will try to protect them.

Angelfish can prove to be truly fascinating aquarium occupants and the likelihood of breeding them successfully is quite high, especially if live food features in their diet. A significant number of color variants have been created, including the platinum form, where the fish are silvery in color, lacking any signs of striping, and golden-yellow variants. There is also another separate species which is offered on occasions, called the deep angelfish (*P. altum*), so called because of its significantly longer dorsal and anal fins. It has proved much harder to persuade this species to spawn, although its general care does not differ from that if its better-known cousin.

⭐ **ANGELFISH**

Pterophyllum scalare
Distribution: Wide-ranging in the Amazon basin
Length: 6in (15cm)
Temperament: Territorial and may prey on small fish
Food: Omnivorous, but prefers live foods
Water temperature: 75-82°F (24-28°C)

➲ Angelfish.
➲➲ Black lace angelfish.

Discus

The similarity between the shape of these fish and the discus used at athletics events is responsible for their common name. Discus have become immensely popular over recent years, as an ever-increasing range of color varieties has been created, but they are not always easy fish to keep, having very specific needs in terms of the water chemistry. This again needs to be soft and acidic, with aquarium peat in the box filter, and blackwater extract in the tank water is advisable too.

It is quite possible to keep discus in groups, providing the tank itself is large enough, and rearing young fish together in this way should ensure that you have at least one compatible pair, which can then be transferred to separate quarters for breeding purposes. Their behavior again provides the best clues to their gender, as there is no obvious way of distinguishing the sexes physically. A pair will start to clean the intended spawning site prior to egg-laying. Rockwork may be chosen for this purpose, although sometimes vegetation is preferred.

The adult fish will stay close to the eggs and then help the fry to hatch about two days after spawning occurs. By five days old, the young discus, which have an elongated body shape at this stage, will be observed feeding on the mucus being secreted on their parents' flanks. Their body shape starts to transform from the age of three months onward.

There are a number of different strains of this species, based on their coloration, known as blue, green and brown, from which today's varieties are descended. There is also a separate species recognized, called the Heckel discus (*S. discus*), usually distinguishable by a wide dark band encircling the body from the dorsal fin down to the anal fin. These fish grow slightly larger, and have acquired a reputation for being harder to spawn successfully.

★ DISCUS

Symphysodon aequifasciatus
Distribution: Tributaries of the Amazon basin
Length: 6in (15cm)
Temperament: Territorial when breeding
Food: Prepared and fresh live foods preferred
Water temperature: 79-86°F (26-30°C)

⬆ Blue discus. ➡ Pigeon's blood discus (*S. aequifasciatus* var.).

Ram

This cichlid is known under a variety of other names, including the butterfly cichlid, a reference to its delicate, wing-like fins. Their small size means that a pair can be kept and bred quite satisfactorily in a relatively small aquarium; sexing is quite straightforward. Males have a significantly larger dorsal fin and are larger than females, and lack the red coloration on their underparts.

Similar water conditions to those recommended for discus suit these fish well. The tank should be well planted in some areas, with rockwork included alongside more open areas for swimming. A submerged clay flowerpot can also be provided, with spawning often occurring there, or sometimes in a depression on the floor of the aquarium. The red eggs will hatch about four days later. The female watches over her brood at this stage, guarding them as far as possible through the first week of their lives. When conditions are suitable, repeated spawnings every month or so may be anticipated.

⭐ RAM

Papiliochromis ramirezi
Distribution: Northern South America, in Colombia and Venezuela
Length: 3in (7.5cm)
Temperament: Males are aggressive toward each other
Food: Live foods of all types preferred
Water temperature: 72–77°F (22–25°C)

These cichlids have been popular with aquarists for more than 50 years.

Malawi golden cichlid

One of the numerous species originating from the lakes of East Africa, this cichlid requires very different water conditions from its South American cousins. These should be medium–hard and alkaline. Sexing is straightforward, as only females display the characteristic golden coloration on the flanks, while mature males are blackish, aside from a lighter stripe running down the sides of the body. A single male should be housed in a tank in the company of several females, rather than with other males, because they are aggressive by nature.

The breeding behavior of this species is fascinating. Females lay in the region of just 30 eggs (usually in the confines of a sheltered cave), compared with the hundreds produced by other cichlids. This is because the eggs receive a high degree of parental care, so there will be a correspondingly high number of fry produced, assuming they were successfully fertilized at the time of laying. The Malawi golden cichlid is a mouth-brooding species; the female collects her eggs and keeps them in her mouth until they hatch, after which the fry dart out, but retreat back there to safety over the course of the next week or so if danger threatens.

⭐ MALAWI GOLDEN CICHLID

Melanochromis auratus
Distribution: Shallow waters of Lake Malawi
Length: 5in (12.5cm)
Temperament: Males are very territorial
Food: Mainly herbivorous
Water temperature: 72-79°F (22-26°C)

Adult males have a very distinctive color pattern, but young males resemble immature females.

ANABANTOIDS

The breeding habits of this group of fish are equally fascinating, and underlie their alternative common group name of bubblenest builders. This is because male fish in most cases create a nest of bubbles of saliva at the surface of the water, where they will watch over their eggs until they hatch. This breeding behavior is possible since most species of anabantoid occur in poorly oxygenated and slow-flowing if not stagnant areas of standing water, such as ditches, rather than fast-flowing rivers that would sweep such nests away.

⬆ Anabantoid distribution.

In order to obtain sufficient oxygen in such waters, these fish are characterized by the presence of what is known as a labyrinth organ on each side of the head, linking with the gills. This organ enables them to gulp atmospheric air and extract oxygen directly from the atmosphere. This adaptation also enables certain species such as climbing perch (*Ctenopoma* sp.) to move across land in search of other areas of water, if their pools start to dry up.

Dwarf gourami

Within this group of fish, there are certain species which can potentially grow to a very large size, notably the gourami (*Osphronemus goramy*) itself, and are typically too large for the home aquarium. The dwarf gourami, however, is very suitable for a community tank setup, and pairs can be recognized quite easily, with females having a much more silvery appearance than males. The water in their aquarium needs to be soft and relatively acid, which means they could be housed with tetras. Barbs are less suitable as tankmates because they are more inclined to nip the gourami's relatively long fins.

A spawning tank for dwarf gouramis and similar species needs to be set up carefully, so that the bubblenest will not be destroyed by the filtration system. Floating plants should be incorporated here, serving as anchorage points that help the male to construct the nest. This can be massive, creating a foam-like appearance reaching up to an inch (2.5cm) above the water surface. After egg-laying has occurred, the male may become more aggressive toward his mate, and so they should be separated at this stage, leaving the male to watch over the bubblenest while the female is transferred back to the aquarium.

The fry hatch quickly, within a couple of days. You need infusoria to rear these and other gouramis at first, because their small mouths mean they cannot consume large particles of food at this stage. A hood over the tank is essential to keep the air temperature constant. The young fish can otherwise become fatally chilled at this stage from breathing cold air via their labyrinth organs. Various color varieties of the dwarf gourami have now been created, including red and blue variants.

★ DWARF GOURAMI

Colisa lalia

Distribution: Northeast India and Bangladesh

Length: 2in (5cm)

Temperament: Not disruptive or aggressive

Food: Omnivorous, based on a diet including small live foods

Water temperature: 72-82°F (22-28°C)

🔼 Neon dwarf gourami.

🔽 Dwarf gourami.

Pearl gourami

The striking pearl-like markings on the flanks of these fish mean they can be identified quite easily. By the time that they are seven months old, males will be identifiable by the red coloration of their underparts. Another change at this stage is that they develop rays on their fins, which provide an irresistible target to fish that engage in fin-nipping, and so their companions need to be chosen carefully. Male pearl gouramis construct a big bubblenest, with females laying a correspondingly large number of eggs—frequently more than 1,000—so that the spawning tank for these fish needs to be suitably spacious, with floating plants providing a framework for the nest. Hatching occurs within a day, the young fish being guarded at first by the male.

✪ PEARL GOURAMI

Trichogaster leeri
Distribution: The Malay Peninsula, to Borneo and Sumatra
Length: Up to 6in (15cm)
Temperament: Males become territorial when breeding
Food: Variety of food, including small live foods
Water temperature: 73-82°F (23-28°C)

➲ All male gouramis tend to have longer and more pointed dorsal fins than females.

➲ Pearl gouramis become increasingly colorful as spawning time approaches.

Kissing gourami

The strange behavior of these fish may look like a sign of affection, but in reality, it appears to be a way of resolving disagreements amicably, without fighting. Locking their fleshy lips together allows these gouramis to engage in a trial of strength, with the weaker individual ultimately backing down. Their large lips are also useful for feeding, as they enable these fish to browse easily on algae. Unfortunately, kissing gouramis may also resort to destroying plants in the aquarium, usually nibbling off the delicate shoots, which ultimately causes the whole plant to die back. Tough, fast-growing vegetation is therefore recommended for their aquarium. Providing greenstuff as part of their diet will help to reduce the risk of plants being nibbled, but if all else fails, plastic plants may have to be used instead.

Visual sexing of kissing gouramis is essentially impossible, until the female swells up with spawn. The male in this case does not generally construct a bubblenest, or watch over the eggs and fry. Instead, the eggs are allowed to float around at the water's surface until they hatch, and as a result, it is a good idea to remove both members of the pair after spawning has occurred, as they may resort to eating them. Infusoria will be required for rearing the young fish once they are free-swimming. As in other cases, a very gentle filtration system should be provided in a spawning tank for these fish.

⭐ KISSING GOURAMI

Helostoma temmincki
Distribution: Southeast Asia
Length: Typically 6-8in (15-20cm)
Temperament: Not overtly aggressive
Food: Omnivorous, including vegetable matter
Water temperature: 72-86°F (22-30°C)

Blue gourami

This particular fish is known under a wide range of different common names, which can create confusion. These included the spotted, two-spot, and three-spot gourami, as well as the hairfin, which is a reference to the hair-like appearance of the pectoral fin. Even the description of blue gourami is not entirely accurate, because gouramis of this color only come from Sumatra. Those occurring elsewhere through the species' range vary in color, with brown and lavender shades being common.

The sexes can be distinguished quite easily, since only males have a pointed dorsal fin. This is significant, because male blue gouramis should be housed separately, since they are likely to prove to be aggressive toward each other. Displays of aggression may also occur in a spawning tank, and so it is important that females have suitable retreats in these surroundings, which can be created by incorporating plastic plants.

The male will often build a big bubblenest which can be up to 10in (25cm) in diameter, and so a relatively large spawning tank is advisable, particularly as females may lay 1,000 eggs or more at a single spawning. The fish should then be separated, with the male being left to guard the nest while the female is transferred back to the main aquarium. It is vital to keep the aquarium covered at first, so the young fry do not become chilled. Allow them adequate space as they grow larger, and do not neglect partial water changes either, to safeguard their health.

✪ BLUE GOURAMI

Trichogaster trichopterus
Distribution: Southeast Asia, including Indonesia
Length: Can be up to 6in (15cm)
Food: Flake and small live foods
Temperament: Mature males are aggressive to each other
Water temperature: 73-82°F (23-28°C)

These gouramis, like related species, may tend to bully smaller companions. Males should be kept separate from each other.

Betta (Siamese fighting fish)

The beauty of the male betta has been greatly enhanced by generations of selective breeding in its native Thailand (formerly known as Siam), where these fish have been kept for centuries, not for their decorative value however, but rather for their fighting prowess. Males must always be kept singly in an aquarium, although they will mix well in these surroundings with other fish. In fact, a male may end up being bullied itself by other tank occupants, who will nip at his long flowing fins. Siamese fighting fish occur in a wide range of colors, although shades of red and blue are perhaps most common. Female bettas are far more placid and can be distinguished easily by their much plainer brownish coloration and less elaborate fins.

Their care is quite straightforward, although pairs should be transferred to a separate spawning tank for breeding purposes. The male fish will create a bubblenest, aided by air from his labyrinth organs as in related species, with the female then being induced to spawn in its vicinity. Sometimes, the nest may be at least partially concealed under floating vegetation at the water's surface.

The female fighting fish releases her eggs in batches, which the male takes to the nest, and this can be a protracted process, lasting over two hours. It will take about two days for the eggs to hatch. The young must be given a suitable fry food as they become free-swimming, and the water quality will need to be monitored and maintained as they grow. It is generally safe to leave the young male fish together until they are about three months old, by which stage, they are likely to be showing signs of aggression toward each other.

⭐ BETTA (SIAMESE FIGHTING FISH)

Betta splendens
Distribution: Southeast Asia
Length: 3in (7.5cm)
Food: Prepared foods and small live foods
Temperament: Males are highly aggressive toward each other
Water temperature: 75-82°F (24-28°C)

A magnificent male betta. Small live foods are very useful in conditioning these fish for breeding purposes.

Paradise fish

These attractive anabantoids may have been introduced to Europe as far back as the 1600s. Fish of similar appearance are described by the English diarist Samuel Pepys. Several color variants have since been documented, including a blue form. Although often considered to be tropical fish, they are actually quite hardy, and so they could have been kept satisfactorily in that era.

Male paradise fish in particular are very attractive, and can be easily recognized by their brighter coloration and longer fins. They are highly territorial as well, and so should be kept on the basis of a single male per tank. Unfortunately, males are also very deter-mined when breeding, and can pursue females relentlessly, often coming into condition before their would-be mates. As a result of the constant harassment, the female may lose condition, and so their aquarium needs to be well planted, to offer her some retreats where she can escape from her would-be partner's attentions.

It is possible to condition paradise fish to breed without too much difficulty, simply by raising the water temperature gradually in the aquarium to the upper limit of the range, and increasing the amount of live food such as whiteworm in their diet at the same time. The male will build a bubblenest in the spawning tank, and here, the female can lay as many as 500 eggs.

⭐ PARADISE FISH

Macropodus opercularis
Distribution: Southern China, Taiwan, Korea, and Vietnam
Length: 4.75 in (12cm)
Food: Variety of prepared foods, and live foods
Temperament: Males are aggressive and can be disruptive
Water temperature: Below 61-82°F (16-28°C)

In warmer areas of the world, paradise fish have been housed successfully in ponds through the summer months.

TOOTHCARPS: LIVEBEARERS AND KILLIFISH

This extensive family includes some of the most widely kept of all tropical fish, being subdivided on the basis of their reproductive habits. Poecilids such as the guppy produce live young whereas the killifish produce eggs. They are all quite small fish, but their requirements in some cases are quite specific, to the extent that this may preclude them from being included as part of a mixed community aquarium.

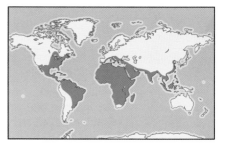

➊ Toothcarp distribution.

Guppy

Few tropical fish have been transformed as strikingly over many generations of selective breeding as the guppy. Today's strains are far removed in appearance from those discovered on Trinidad by the Rev. John Guppy in 1865. In fact, fish corresponding to the wild form of the guppy are rarely available, usually being in the hands of specialist breeders of livebearers, and today considered exceedingly nondescript in appearance.

There are now 12 basic divisions of fancy varieties, characterized by differences in the shape and size of the dorsal and tail fins, with prescribed standards being laid down for judging purposes. Those guppies that have projections extending from the top and/or bottom of the tail fins are known as sword-tailed. Where the tail is simply greatly enlarged into a triangular shape, the fish are sometimes described as delta-tailed. The coloration of guppies today is equally variable, ranging from yellow through reds to blues and purple. Males in all cases are smaller and much more colorful than females. Some of the most impressive forms are patterned varieties such as the snakeskin or cobra forms.

The most striking effect can be created by setting up an aquarium for a particular variety and color of guppy. Unfortunately, however, it seems that the commercial breeding of some varieties over many years has adversely affected the vigor of these strains. A combination of factors is often blamed, ranging from excessive inbreeding to the overuse of antibiotics.

It can be harder to determine whether a female guppy has an extended or rounded tail, compared with a male, but those of an extended tail strain have bigger and more colorful tails compared with those having rounded tails. Most serious exhibition breeders maintain at least two separate lines, which they can cross on occasions to maintain the vigor of their fish.

Breeding guppies on this scale represents a major undertaking in terms of the number of tanks and other equipment that will be required, but these fish represent an excellent introduction to the world of fish breeding. Females will give birth readily, often every four weeks or so, and provided that the mother is kept apart from her young after giving birth, there is every likelihood that the majority will survive without problems. If they are left in an aquarium, then only if it is well planted is there a likelihood that even a few will survive being eaten through the critical early days of life.

⭐ GUPPY

Poecilia reticulata
Distribution: Region north of the Amazon
Length: Males 1.25in (3cm); females 2in (5cm) or bigger
Food: Omnivorous, with some vegetable matter
Temperament: Highly social, nonaggressive
Water temperature: 64-82°F (18-28°C)

Swordtail

Again, the domesticated forms of this livebearer are far more colorful than their wild counterparts, which are rarely available today. While wild swordtails tend to be green in color, shades of red and orange usually predominate in aquarium fish, often set against black markings. There have also been a number of changes in the appearance of their fins, with some varieties having an enlarged dorsal, often known as a hi-fin.

Although these fish are named after the sword-like extension on the bottom of the caudal fin of males, strains with a similar enlargement on the top of this fin are also now established, being described as lyre-tails. Mating a male fish with a normal tail to a lyre-tailed female can breed these. Approximately half of the resulting young will themselves have lyre tails.

Since much of the early development of swordtails occurred in Germany, so today's color varieties are often named after German cities where they were created. The Wiesbaden swordtail for example has black flanks, with red or green underparts, while the Berlin strain is red with black spots. In this latter case however, Berlin swordtails are always mated not to each other, but to red individuals, in order to prevent the development of tumors that are otherwise likely to afflict their offspring. Some of the swordtail variants that are now being bred owe their existence to cross-breeding with platies (*Xiphophorus maculatus*).

Although swordtails can be housed as part of a community aquarium, they should not be kept with fish that will nip the tips of their swords. You should also avoid keeping more than one male swordtail alongside a group of females, because the weaker individual will be bullied. If you are not interested in breeding these fish however, a group of four or five males will often live happily together when housed apart from females, so there is little rivalry between them. In a group of young fish, it is the male that grows the longest sword-like extension on his tail that will be the dominant individual in the group. As with

⊕ Natural neighbors in a Central American coastal stream, swordtails and a horse-face loach feed on fine particles of food at the bottom of the tank.

other livebearers, using a separate breeding tank will give the best chance of raising the majority of the brood successfully, which may number as many as 200 fry.

⭐ SWORDTAIL

Xiphophorus helleri
Distribution: Mexico to Honduras
Length: Males up to 4in (10cm) including swordlike tail. Females are slightly larger overall
Food: Prepared foods and small live foods
Temperament: Males can be aggressive
Water temperature: 70-77°F (21-25°C)

Southern platy

This species is also sometimes known as the maculatus platy, because of its scientific name. Even in the wild, these fish display considerable variation in their coloration, so it is therefore not surprising that more than 30 distinctive strains have now been created. Males in all cases can be distinguished by their smaller size, and the adaptation of the anal fin into the tubelike gonopodium that is used for mating purposes.

Although the color of wild southern platies tends to be olive-brown, some individuals do show traces of reddish coloration, and this is now a common feature in domestic strains. Typical colors encountered in these platies vary from shades of yellowish-orange through red to blue and black. Coral platies show the darkest red coloration.

In other cases, black markings are evident, as in the case of tuxedo strains, similar to those recognized in swordtails. Tuxedo platies have mat black coloration on the sides of the bodies, which does not extend to the fins. In contrast, wagtail platies have black fins, aside from the ventral and anal fins on the underside of the body.

Dark markings on or near the tail are a common feature of many varieties of platy. Moon platies for example, have a prominent circular marking at the base of the tail, in the vicinity of the caudal peduncle, where it joins the body; the simple crescent marking takes the form of a curved black line in this region, while the comet has dark edges present on the top and bottom of its caudal fin, hence the alternative common name, moonfish.

★ SOUTHERN PLATY

Xiphophorus maculatus
Distribution: Mexico south to Belize and Guatemala
Length: Males measure up to 1.5in (4cm); females 2.5in (6cm)
Food: Flake and other prepared food, plus live food
Temperament: Not aggressive, even toward each other
Water temperature: 64-77°F (18-25°C)

Brilliantly colored and easy to breed, small
wonder that this fish has become so popular.

Where there are dark spots over the entire body, the fish is known
as a pepper and salt platy. The use of a color food can help to improve
the contrast in the appearance of such fish, especially where red
coloration is involved, just as it can with swordtails.

The lack of aggression among platies means they are relatively
easy to accommodate and breed, although again, newly produced
young are vulnerable to being eaten at first, unless they are kept
apart from larger fish. They can be fed initially on a livebearer fry
food, and then powdered flake can be gradually introduced to
their diet. This is easily prepared by rubbing it gently through
your fingers and dropping it onto the water surface.

Variegated platy

These platies are often yellowish-orange in color, and are also
known as the variatus platy, thanks to the dark bars present on the
sides of their bodies. Unfortunately, repeated crossings to southern
platies mean that purebred stock is hard to acquire, but true variegated platies are slightly larger in size, with a more slender appearance overall. There is a strain with an enlarged dorsal fin, but the
choices are more limited than with the southern species. The sunset platy, for example, has a yellow dorsal and a red tail fin, with
the body itself being bluish. Yellow coloration predominates to a
greater extent in the marigold strain, extending from the dorsal fin
along the back, while the tail and lower half of the body are
orange. The Hawaiian form has a mat black body, while the color of
its fins corresponds to that of the sunset platy, except that the dorsal fin of females is usually paler in color.

Although variegated platies are less commonly available, their
requirements are the same as their southern cousin, and breeding
details are similar as well. They may have between 50 and 100 fry
every month or so, when well-fed and housed in slightly alkaline and

medium-hard water conditions. They are actually relatively adaptabl
in terms of their water chemistry requirements.

Xiphophorus variatus
Distribution: Atlantic side of Mexico
Length: Males measure up to 2.25in
(5.5cm); females 2.75in (7cm)
Food: Flake and other prepared food,
plus live food
Temperament: Not aggressive, even
toward each other
Water temperature: 64-77°F (18-25°C)

Black molly

The origins of this particular fish are cloaked in mystery, althoug
it is immensely popular among aquarists, with its mat black col
oration looking especially striking when set alongside the reddis
coloration of swordtails in the same aquarium. These fish ca
make a good combination. Both require similar water conditions
with the addition of marine salt to their tank water, at a concen
tration of approximately one teaspoonful per gallon (3.8 liters)
Deducting 10 percent of the volume to allow for the decor i
often prudent. The salt will help to guard against fungus, bein
particularly important if the mollies have been previously house
in brackish water.

What is especially interesting is that black mollies do not occu
anywhere in the wild. They are thought to be a color variant whic
arose in the wild sphenops molly, and may also have been develope
by crossings with another species, the sailfin molly (*P. velifera*).

The upturned mouth of these fish indicates they will regularly fee
at the water's surface, but they are also valuable in the aquarium fo
grazing on algae. Take particular care when choosing black mollies a
the outset, as they have acquired a justified reputation for sufferin
from white spot (*see* pages 134–5), not to mention piscine tubercu
losis (*see* page 130).

Females may have broods of as many as 80 youngsters, and gener
ally, most mollies are more tolerant of their offspring than other live
bearers. But if they are sharing their accommodation with other fish
the young mollies will be equally vulnerable, especially if the tank i
not densely planted. In contrast to many other livebearers, they hav

a relatively slow rate of growth as well, so that a separate spawning tank that can double as rearing quarters is recommended.

⭐ BLACK MOLLY

Poecilia sphenops var

Distribution: This variety does not occur in the wild. Ancestral form ranges from Texas to Colombia in South America

Length: 3.25in (8cm), females often slightly larger

Food: Omnivorous, but must have vegetable matter

Temperament: Nonaggressive, shoaling fish

Water temperature: 64-82°F (18-28°C)

Lyretail killifish

Unfortunately, killifish like the beautiful lyretail are not really suitable for a community aquarium, as their requirements are quite specific. They can be encouraged to spawn without too much difficulty. They inhabit temporary areas of water created by rainfall, not surprisingly, they need very soft and acidic water conditions. Their aquarium should have a base of aquarium peat, while the addition of approximately one teaspoonful of marine salt per gallon (3.8 liters) of water is advised.

Males are especially beautiful, developing a characteristic lyre-shaped tail, with longer rays top and bottom, as well as prominent red markings on their fins. The body too is covered in bright red spots.

Unlike many killifish, the lyretail, also known as the Cape Lopaz lyretail because of the area in West Africa where it was first recorded, spawns among vegetation. Alternatively, a pair may use a spawning mop in their quarters for this purpose, and afterward, they should be transferred back to their permanent tank. Hatching takes about two weeks, and the young fish can then be reared in the spawning tank. They may live for three years or so.

In the case of other killifish that lay in the substrate, let this dry out slowly, leave it dry for about two weeks, then flood it again. This should result in some of the eggs hatching, although it is worthwhile repeating this process two or three times. By ensuring that not all the young hatch at once in the wild, there is a greater probability that at least one group will survive long enough to spawn successfully themselves. Killifish eggs encased in mud under these conditions may remain viable for two years or more.

⊙ Amazonian floodplain. Corydoras spawn at the start of the wet season, so that lowering the water level and then topping up the aquarium with fresh, dechlorinated water can serve as a breeding trigger.

CATFISH

There are more than 2,400 different species of catfish, divided into 34 families, comprising the order Siluriformes, and they display a tremendous diversity in form and size. Barbels can help to identify catfish, but not all species are equipped with these sensory projections around the mouth. In fact, most of the features that these fish have in common are found in their skeletal structure, and are therefore not obvious in live specimens.

One very unusual trait seen in some of these fish is their ability to use their swimbladder to vibrate and emit sounds, which have been described in various ways, from squeaking and croaking to talking. Many catfish can also actually hear sounds as well—an important sensory refinement in the muddy waters that many species inhabit in the wild. As far as the aquarist is concerned, no other group of fish shows such an amazing diversity in size, ranging from just 1.5in (3.5cm) in the case of the pygmy catfish (*Corydoras pygmaeus*) up to giants of the group such as the wels catfish, which may grow to a length of at least 16.5ft (5m).

Corydoras spawn at the start of the wet season, so that lowering the water level and then topping up the aquarium with fresh, dechlorinated water can serve as a breeding trigger.

Bronze corydoras

The attractive Corydoras catfish are very popular occupants of a typical community aquarium, thanks in part to their small size. They are also very easy to keep in these surroundings. The bronze corydoras, so called because of the sheen on its body, is especially popular, and occurs in several different color forms, of which the most common is undoubtedly an albino variant, being white in color with red eyes. Check the barbels around the mouths of these fish. Should these appear to be shortening, this suggests that the substrate is dirty, causing the barbels to become infected.

Bronze corydoras have a remarkable breeding cycle. Adopting a T-shaped position for mating, the female actually swallows the male's sperm directly from his vent. The sperm passes immediately through her digestive system, without being attacked and destroyed by enzymes, to emerge through her vent to fertilize eggs clasped in her pelvic fins. She will then conceal these adhesive eggs beneath a rock or in a similar locality, with the fry hatching about six days later.

★ BRONZE CORYDORAS

Corydoras aeneus
Distribution: Much of the northern part of South America
Length: 2.75in (7cm)
Food: Eats sinking pellets and live food readily
Temperament: Social, agreeing well in groups
Water temperature: 70-79°F (20-26°C)

Several naturally occurring color forms are known, including Peru green stripe and Aeneus black.

Leopard corydoras

The markings of these Corydoras are highly individual, with a series of dark blackish spots, sometimes coalescing together to form lines. There is also a more definite dark line running along each side of the body, roughly level with the eyes. Identification is not entirely straightforward, however, as they can easily be confused with *C. tri-lineatus*, although this Peruvian species has larger, coarser spots. Sex determination is also difficult, but since they are social by nature, obtaining a small group should ensure you have at least one pair.

Unlike some catfish, Corydoras are not strictly nocturnal, and will feed during the day, but they prefer shaded conditions. They are also well adapted to survive in waters with low oxygen content, because they can breathe atmospheric air directly, gulping this from the water surface. The gas is absorbed through the wall of the hind gut.

Corydoras julii
Distribution: Brazilian tributaries of the lower Amazon
Length: 2in (5cm)
Food: Eats sinking pellets and live food readily
Temperament: Social, lives well in groups
Water temperature: 70-79°F (20-26°C)

The ventral fins of male Corydoras are usually narrower in shape than those of females.

Spotted pleco

These placid catfish can grow to a relatively large size, making them unsuitable for smaller community aquariums. They are sometimes also called suckermouths, because of the sucker-like action of their lips, which means they can anchor themselves firmly on to rockwork or plants. This helps them to maintain their position in a fast-flowing current. Their mouth also contains strong teeth, so they can rasp algae or even fragments of submerged wood, which form part of their diet.

A unique feature of this group of catfish, not seen in any other vertebrate grouping, is the way in which they can control the amount of light entering their eyes. Rather than altering the diameter of the pupil, suckermouth catfish have a special lobe that acts rather like a filter, being shifted across the iris to block out light when necessary. These catfish are relatively secretive by nature, and need a sheltered locality in the aquarium, such as bogwood where they can rest largely out of sight. They tend to be most active after dark.

Hypostomus punctatus
Distribution: Southern Brazil
Length: Up to 12in (30cm)
Food: Herbivorous diet, plenty of vegetable matter
Temperament: Not aggressive
Water temperature: 72-82°F (22-28°C)

The size of these catfish makes them suitable companions for larger New World cichlids such as angelfish.

Pleco

In spite of its potentially large size, the pleco which is also some-times known simply as the plec, is an easy species to care for, being relatively unfussy about water chemistry, although it will not thrive when there is a build-up of nitrogenous waste. Plecs are ideal com-panions for larger, nonaggressive fish, but they will soon outgrow the average aquarium. Bogwood again is essential in their quarters, helping to provide additional fiber in their diet. Plecs that are kept without the opportunity to rasp this type of wood may not thrive.

The taxonomy of these sucker-mouthed catfish is confused, and it is likely that several different forms may be offered under this general name. There is an albino variant that is well established, as well as a piebald form, displaying colored and white patches on its body. This should not be confused with the snow king plec (*Liposarcus anisisti*), which has variable white spots on its body. Their care is very similar, although the snow king plec only grows to about 16in (41cm) or so.

Although breeding is unlikely to be achieved in the confines of an aquarium, female plecs are known to lay their eggs in hollows in riverbanks, where the male guards them. The young fry feed on the body mucus of the adult fish at first, which might help to give them some early immunity from infection, in addition to nutrients.

⭐ PLECO

Hypostomus plecostomus
Distribution: Surinam
Length: Up to 24in (60cm)
Food: Herbivorous diet, plenty of vegetable matter
Temperament: Not aggressive
Water temperature: 72-82°F (22-28°C)

OTHER FISH

There are a number of other groups of fish that are popular aquari-um occupants, but do not fit in any of the foregoing categories. Loaches are prominent among these, and they form part of the large and diverse order Cypriniformes, being subdivided into four families.

Kuhli loach

There are two distinctive subspecies of the kuhli (or coolie) loach, which can be separated on the basis of their banding. The Sumatran form typically has fewer than 15 black bands on its body, compared with the more widely distributed nominate race, which is more intensely colored with narrow redder bands, although the black areas do not encircle the body. Unfortunately, once released into an aquarium, kuhli loaches are soon likely to disappear from sight. They will burrow into the substrate, or hide away beneath rockwork and other tank decor, only tending to emerge when the tank is in darkness.

Kuhli loaches should be kept in groups, and in view of their secretive natures, it is not uncommon for a pair to spawn successfully, their eggs being scattered around the floor. Take particular care when netting these fish, as they have a small spine located beneath each eye. This defensive mechanism is designed to stick in the mouth of a would-be predator, and the spine will dig into a net in a similar fashion, being hard to dislodge as a result.

★ KUHLI LOACH

Pangio kuhli
Distribution: Malay peninsula and nearby islands
Length: 4in (10cm)
Food: Omnivorous, but favors small sinking live foods
Temperament: Secretive, inoffensive
Water temperature: 75-86°F (24-30°C)

Clown loach

The striped patterning of these fish has led to the alternative common name, tiger loach. They can grow quite large, rapidly outstripping other tank occupants. Their coloration varies between individuals, the orange areas being brighter in some cases than others, but this is not a means of sexing these fish. Males may be identified, however, especially once they are larger, by their bigger caudal fin. In the wild, these fish spawn after heavy rainfall, which turns the rivers into raging torrents. It is hard to replicate these conditions in the aquarium, but an influx of fresh, soft water and a power filter may serve to trigger this behavior.

These loaches can be kept in a group. Do not worry unduly if you see one of these fish lying on its side, often not moving, which could suggest that it is dying. Such behavior is quite normal in these loaches, and indicates that the fish is simply resting. Clown loaches, like the kuhli loach, also have spikes below the eyes.

★ CLOWN LOACH

Botia macracantha
Distribution: Indonesia, Borneo and Sumatra
Length: 12in (30cm)
Food: Omnivorous, often likes live foods
Temperament: Social with its own kind
Water temperature: 75-86°F (24-30°C)

Clown loaches are often more active during the day than other loaches.

Chinese algae eater

In spite of their name, these fish do not originate from China. Their alternative common name of sucking loach is misleading as well, since they are not considered to be true loaches either. The extensible mouth means that the sucking loach lives up to its second name, however, as it can anchor itself on to stones and bogwood, even in the face of strong water currents. These fish are unusual in having evolved a way to use their gills effectively when they are anchored by their sucker mouth. They have a small hole on the top of their gill covers for this purpose.

Chinese algae eaters can prove valuable in curbing the growth of algae within an aquarium, in association with other measures such as reviewing the lighting arrangements. Spawning in the home aquarium does not appear to have been achieved, but these fish are bred commercially, with the brightly colored golden form having become the most popular. They are probably not an ideal choice for a community tank, partly because they grow rather large. In addition, Chinese algae eaters will sometimes attach themselves to the sides of other fish, feeding on their protective layer of body mucus and leaving them more vulnerable to infection as a result. They are not generally aggressive by nature.

★ CHINESE ALGAE EATER

Gyrinocheilus aymonieri
Distribution: Thailand
Length: Up to 10.5in (27cm)
Food: Omnivorous but must have vegetable matter
Temperament: Become much more territorial as they grow larger
Water temperature: 70-82°F (21-28°C)

CHAPTER 4

Stocking and Maintaining the Aquarium

By leaving the aquarium operating for a few days without putting the fish in place, this ensures that conditions will ultimately be better when you do obtain them. This applies equally with either a coldwater or tropical tank. The bacterial population in the filter bed, for example, will be more numerous, and the plants will settle down.

A t the same time, you can ensure the lighting system—and heating too if necessary—are functioning properly. This interval also gives you the opportunity to finalize the list of fish that appeal to you, so that you can search out which of them are available in your locality.

BUYING FISH

There are a number of different aspects to consider when deciding on the fish for your aquarium, and much obviously depends on the type of fish that appeal to you. There are two basic choices, with probably the most popular option being what is often described as a community aquarium, housing a range of different fish. (The other main alternative is a single-species aquarium.) It is important that you consider the natural behavior of the fish. Some, such as the red-

◐ Examining the new purchases at the shop; better to find problems there than at home.

① SCHOOLING CONCERNS

While some fish are relatively solitary, many of those living especially in the middle area of water, such as rasboras and tetras, are social by nature, and they will not thrive in an aquarium if kept just singly or in twos. This will also have a detrimental effect on the overall well being of the other aquarium occupants, because when kept in very small numbers, these fish often prove to be more nervous than normal, darting around in the hope of avoiding danger. In a school, however, where there are effectively more eyes to detect any threat, they prove to be more placid by nature.

⊖ The water in this newly set-up tank, containing just a few fish, is cloudy, but efficient filtration clears it for the green swordtails in just a few days. This initial cloudiness does not spell disaster. It is partly the result of a time lag before the filtration processes kick in, but mostly just substrate particles in suspension.

bellied piranha (*Serrasalmus nattereri*), can be too aggressive. Others, such as the tinfoil barb (*Barbus schwanenfeldi*), may become too large.

Although it is possible to generalize to some extent on the temperaments of fish, they are individuals. Some reputedly tolerant individuals may be more aggressive than anticipated. Often, it can be a matter of a similarity in color, with a fish of another species being seen as a would-be rival. Certain fish, such as the red-tailed black shark (*Labeo bicolor*), can be quite amenable to other fish as part of a mixed community aquarium but highly aggressive toward others of their own kind and toward related species such as the red-finned shark (*Labeo erythrurus*), especially as they grow older.

Rather than keeping a mixed collection of fish, some people prefer to have a single-species aquarium. Such an aquarium often comprises pairs of large fish, especially for breeding purposes, where the presence of companions can prove to be disruptive. Typical candidates for this type of setup include discus (*Symphysodon* sp.) as well as other cichlids such as oscars (*Astronotus ocellatus*), which can also become quite tame.

Often sold as young fish, such cichlids will usually grow fast under ideal conditions, and so keeping a group together will therefore demand a large aquarium. If having more than two fish together appeals to you, then you could have a single-species setup comprising a school of smaller fish. Livebearers, particularly guppies (*Poecilia reticulata*), have been bred in a wide range of fancy varieties and are ideal for this purpose. Keeping a school of these fish

on their own—especially the more colorful males—can create a stunning impression as they shimmer under the lights.

Finally, environmental conditions will also dictate your choice to an extent. Clearly, goldfish are not recommended for inclusion in a heated aquarium, as they require coldwater conditions. Water chemistry also imposes restraints on your choice. Rift Valley cichlids, for example, would not be suitable company for tetras for this reason.

There are various options when it actually comes to obtaining the fish themselves. Most people will visit aquatic stores in their locality, to see what is available. The choice here is fairly constant, although there may be some seasonal variations. If you are looking for the widest choice within a group or any particularly unusual fish (catfish, for example), then you may need to track down a more specialist outlet. These can usually be located easily through advertisements in fish keeping magazines.

All reputable dealers will quarantine their fish to allow them to recover from the effects of the trip to the store and ensure that they are healthy. Even so, it pays to look carefully before buying any fish. First impressions on entering a store are important, with well-labeled tanks being a good sign. Another positive tip-off is membership of a recognized trade association, usually indicated by a logo on the door.

THE TRAFFIC LIGHT SYSTEM

Some stores use the so-called "traffic light" system to help you gain some insight into the needs of unfamiliar fish. Those that have green dots associated with their name are suitable for a community aquarium, whereas fish whose requirements may be more specialized can be identified by the presence of yellow spots. Difficult or antisocial species are highlighted by red. This, of course, only reveals part of the story, so do not hesitate to ask staff for further advice in a particular case.

When assessing whether to buy any fish, it is important to look closely at all those in the tank. Fish diseases spread through the water, and if you notice one or two black mollies in a tank showing signs of the parasitic disease known as ich or white spot (see pages 134–5), for example, bear in mind that even healthy-looking fish sharing their quarters are at risk of becoming infected. In addition, acquiring mollies out of this tank is like to bring these microscopic parasites home in the water, introducing the infection to your new aquarium. It is therefore essential to buy only from tanks where all the fish appear lively and healthy.

Signs of disease

Some types of fish are more susceptible to certain diseases than others. In the case of cichlids, for example, so-called "hole-in-the-head disease" is a particular problem associated with discus (*Symphysodon* spp.), so familiarize yourself with any particular problems that may be linked with the fish that interest you. Ulcers anywhere on a fish's body are serious, especially because these areas can often provide a means for fungal diseases to attack. Loss of scales, which can sometimes arise from rough handling, can also lead on to fungal infections, especially if a fish has been under stress.

The condition of the fins is also important, because these can provide an indication of water quality, especially in the case of those fish with long, flowing fins. There is again a risk that these could become infected, especially with fungus, as a result of any damage. Even so, provided there are no obvious signs of infection, there is no reason as to why the fins will not regenerate fully, once the fish are established in a new aquarium with better water conditions.

Any abnormalities in the way a fish swims can be potentially serious. They can be signs of dropsy, particularly if the scales appear raised on the body. Fancy varieties of goldfish are especially susceptible to swim-bladder disorders that affect their buoyancy, causing them to swim at an abnormal angle in the water. There is no cure

for this condition, so fish that are affected should be avoided.

In the case of catfish, look closely at the barbels, which are the sensory projections around the mouth. These can become damaged thanks to poor environmental conditions and again, opportunistic infections can then develop here. These are often more common in those catfish which spend their time on or near to the floor of their quarters, such as *Corydoras* spp., compared with those which inhabit the upper reaches in the tank.

⬤ The barbels of this bronze corydoras (*Coryodoras aeneus*) are undamaged and healthy, a positive sign of overall wellbeing for catfish.

You can often gain further insight into the management of the store by the way the fish are caught. Ideally, the catching nets should be kept in a disinfectant solution, to minimize the risk of diseases being spread from one tank to another. Staff will usually go to great lengths to catch the fish that customer's request, but try to avoid unnecessary disruption by being very specific about your requirements. Incidentally, it is largely for ease of viewing the fish and catching them that most store tanks are relatively bare of furnishings.

Fish are typically sold in tough plastic bags, with oxygen added to them, but before the bag is sealed, ask to carry out a close check on the fish. Concentrate on the eyes at this stage: occasionally fish only develop one eye, but this can be hard to spot until they turn their body toward you, and they are often adept at keeping this disability hidden. You can also look at close quarters for any signs of scale damage or lumps that may not have been evident previously.

When you are happy with your choice, the plastic bag containing the fish can be transferred to a paper bag or box, so the fish are in relatively darkness in transit. Recent advances in the design of bags for carrying fish, such as square corners to ensure that the fish cannot become trapped, have made transport less stressful for them.

PURCHASE POINTERS

- No obvious damage to fins or scales.
- Both eyes present and of equal size.
- No growth resembling cotton wool, indicating fungal disease.
- No abnormal white spots.
- No swellings on the body.
- Fish swim normally, not rubbing repeatedly against tank decor.
- Color of the fish: this can sometimes be a significant indicator of their state of health, but bear in mind that if the lighting conditions are very bright above the tank, this can cause them to appear paler than usual. Loss of color can be linked with illness, particularly if the fish are thin, which may be suggestive of piscine tuberculosis (see page 130).

◑ Visiting an aquarium shop is—depending on the kind of shop—a way of getting inspired about your own aquarium layout. Most shops will try to present the fish as attractively as possible, as in this fancy goldfish setup.

> **① SENSIBLE MEASURES**
>
> **Never tip any aquarium water down the kitchen sink because of the slight risk of harmful bacteria that could contaminate these surroundings. It is also sensible to wear plastic gloves for the same reason, particularly if you have any cuts on your hand or if you might have been exposed to chemicals that could prove harmful to the aquarium occupants themselves.**

> **COPING WITH LONG TRIPS**
>
> **You might be concerned about the temperature in the bag falling if the trip home is likely to last several hours. This is not necessarily harmful to fish, because the change is gradual, as can occur in the wild, and if they are carefully reacclimatized on arrival, they should not suffer any long-term effects. If you are worried, however, you can buy a warming pack that can be placed next to the bag, emitting gentle heat to maintain the temperature within. Stores selling camping equipment often sell these, being marketed primarily to keep one's hands warm.**

All fish at once?

There are two opinions about whether to buy all the fish for a community aquarium at the outset. This approach does mean that the fish can all settle down at once, which will be less disturbing for all the tank occupants than adding individuals over time. In addition, you lessen the likelihood of problems arising if you can obtain the fish from a single source. The major drawback of this method is that it places much more of a strain on the filter system, especially if you are relying mainly on biological filtration. The detrimental effects can be minimized to a great extent by careful management, however. This will entail more frequent water changes and monitoring at the outset, until the filter bed is mature.

When you take the fish home, travel back directly, so they are not in their bags for longer than is necessary. Keep the bags upright, preferably standing in a box on the floor behind one of the front seats, so that the fish will not be splashed around on the way. Always plan to go straight home, rather than leaving the fish in a locked car for any length of time, because fish can overheat and rapidly die if they are exposed to direct sunlight in these surroundings.

It is important that the aquarium has been prepared for the arrival of the fish in advance, with the water temperature established at the appropriate level. The bags containing the fish should then be carefully transferred to the aquarium, being left to float here on the surface for approximately 20 minutes, in the case of tropical species.

This provides an opportunity for the temperature of the water in the bags to match that within the aquarium itself. This is less significant in the case of coldwater fish because their water is unheated, but it can be recommended if the weather outside has been cold.

Especially if you have a number of bags, then clearly you cannot simply tip them straight into the aquarium, because the additional water will cause it to overflow. In any case, try to minimize the volume of water that you transfer because of the risk of introducing potentially harmful disease-causing microbes. It is much better simply to net each of the fish in turn, and then lift out the bag and discard the water down an outside drain.

⊙ Some fish such as loaches can become caught up in catching nets thanks to spines below their eyes, which can also puncture thin plastic bags. They need to be transferred from nets with particular care.

Netting and release

Nets to catch aquarium fish are sold in various sizes, and it may be useful to have at least two different sizes available, with the smaller size being useful to remove fish directly from a bag, while the other can be used in the aquarium itself. The depth of the net is as significant as its width. A shallow net means that a fish is more likely to be able to leap out, so as a precautionary measure, always place your other hand over the top of the net as you lift it out of the water.

It is often a good idea to move much of the rockwork and similar decor in an aquarium when catching fish. Otherwise—especially when you are using a net—this can be easily knocked over, and could injure tank occupants as well as damaging the aquarium equipment or the tank itself.

Not all fish are as easily caught as others, and bottom-dwellers can be particularly elusive. Kuhli loaches (*Pangio kuhli*) are especially adept at avoiding capture, slipping through the smallest gaps out of sight, thanks to their eel-like shape. If the undergravel filter is not placed flat on the floor of the aquarium, these fish may even retreat under here. It may actually be better to try to catch them in a bag rather than using a net, because they have spines on the body, close to their eyes,

---

⚠ HANDLING FISH

Fish need to be handled very carefully if they fall out of a net on to the ground. Never attempt to pick up a fish with dry hands, because this is likely to damage the protective layer of mucus that covers the body and protects the scales. As a result, the fish may then develop an infection here, which could ultimately lead on to the development of a life-threatening ulcer. Try to persuade the fish to flip into the wet net instead. It is obviously important that you transfer the fish back to its surroundings as soon as possible, and in most cases, even if the fish has fallen some distance on to the floor, it will be uninjured.

which they raise if threatened. As a result, they can easily become stuck in the fine material of the net itself. This defensive mechanism has evolved to prevent these fish being swallowed easily, as the spines can be erected to stick into tissue as well, causing a would-be predator to retch and seek to eject its intended meal out of its mouth.

When attempting to catch an elusive fish, allow the bag to drift down into the tank, and try to steer the fish into the opening. After that, you can lift it out of the water, carefully tipping back much of the water. This technique may also be useful when attempting to catch tall-bodied fish such as angelfish (*Pterophyllum* spp.), whose shape means they may not fit easily into a standard-sized net, particularly as they grow larger.

Once the fish have been introduced to the aquarium, allow them to settle down without immediately turning on the lights. It is better to allow them to adjust to their new environment in relatively darkened surroundings. Similarly, it is not a good idea to feed them immediately, as they are unlikely to be hungry at this stage. Leave them to settle down for a few hours, and then only offer them a very small amount of food, because if this is not eaten, it will just pollute the water.

CATCHING TIPS

When using a net, rely on stealth to catch fish. Dragging a net behind a fish is rarely satisfactory, because the fish can easily dart away, while the resistance of the water will hold the net back. Instead, drop the net beneath the fish, so that you can scoop it up from beneath, catching it unawares. It may help to bait the surface of the water with a little food, in the hope of drawing the fish up to the surface, away from their hiding places, so that catching them should be easier.

Early vigilance

In the early stages, keep a close watch on the fish to ensure that they remain healthy. It is important to be prepared to remove any individuals that appear off-color, as a precaution against spreading disease to the other occupants of the tank. Investing in a relatively small acrylic aquarium for this purpose is therefore a good idea. Even if your fish do not fall sick, this can serve as a useful quarantine tank for future purchases.

Once the aquarium is set up and functioning well, never be tempted simply to add more fish to it without keeping them isolated for a week or so at first, to ensure that they themselves are healthy and feeding properly. Dealing with any disease in an established aquarium will be much harder and more time-consuming than taking steps to avoid the introduction of sick fish in the first instance.

❶ ... And a little net like the one opposite isn't much use for catching some of the larger catfish or cichlids like this solid citizen, *Herichthys carpinte*. It's common sense, but in an emergency the proper size net may be important to have to hand.

A spare tank can also be useful for emergencies, in case one of the existing members of the aquarium is being badly bullied, or if some of the fish look as if they are likely to breed. An undertank-heating pad with a thermostat will be needed for heating the water, in the case of tropical fish, while the filtration system can consist of a sponge filter, which is ideal when fish are breeding.

Fish are most likely to fall ill when they are moved to new surroundings, as a result of the stress involved.

Buying young fish

❶ An isolation tank will help to prevent diseases being introduced to an established aquarium.

Starting out with young fish can help to prevent initial disappointments. Although goldfish rank among the longest-lived of all aquarium fish, with a life expectancy of up to 40 years, many of the smaller tropical species in particular have short lives, often of just 12-18 months.

Another advantage of starting out with smaller, immature fish is that bullying is less likely to arise at the outset. You need to take particular care if obtaining an adult pair of cichlids such as oscars (*Astronotus ocellatus*), which may already have spawned satisfactorily in aquarium surroundings. It will usually take longer for the female to adjust to new surroundings, and so initially she will be less keen to accept the male's advances. He is likely to respond by harrying her increasingly, with the result that she actually starts to lose condition. By this stage, you will need to separate the pair, transferring the male fish elsewhere for a few weeks so the female can settle without further molestation, before cautiously reintroducing them at a later stage. With personality fish like these, another advantage of buying young fish is that they can be tamed more easily, when obtained young.

Once you have introduced the fish to the aquarium, you will spend time watching them, but be sure to actually count them every day as well, to ensure that none has disappeared. This is particularly important with schooling fish, since the absence of one from the group may be easily overlooked. But if it

⚠ LIFESPAN WARNING

Adult guppies may look very attractive, but by this stage, they will probably only have a few months left to live. Many fish keepers are inevitably disappointed and upset that their fish do not survive for long, but this is actually to be expected. If you want to avoid this situation as far as possible, it will be better to buy a few mature female guppies, which will almost inevitably be carrying young, and then allow these youngsters to grow on in your aquarium in due course. The drawback in this case, however, is that you are unlikely to be able to predict the color or appearance of these fish.

COPING WITH A CRISIS

If a problem has arisen, and you experience widespread mortality among your fish, refer back to the store where you bought them. Most stores are sympathetic in this situation, but are likely to want a sample of the aquarium water to check before reaching any firm conclusions. Telephone the store manager without delay, to raise your concerns, rather than simply turning up unannounced at a time when the store may be busy.

has died, then it is important to locate its body, before it can start to decompose and threaten the water quality for its former tankmates.

FEEDING AND TYPES OF NUTRIENTS

The constituents of a fish's diet are similar to our own. They utilize carbohydrates as a source of energy, and these comprise 20-40 percent of commercial dry foods. Fats (lipids) represent a more concentrated source of energy that can be stored in the body; fat stores can sustain fish when food becomes scarce. These reserves are normally reduced and replenished according to needs, but aquarium fish can become obese if they are allowed to feed in an unrestricted fashion. This is partly because they need to expend relatively little energy in seeking food.

Although fish are often classified as herbivorous or carnivorous, most are omnivorous. They are opportunistic, eating whatever is available. In some areas, particularly temperate waters or regions that undergo marked changes in water level, their diets can vary significantly through the year. This in turn can affect behavior. In temperate areas, for example, an increasing supply of aquatic invertebrates in the spring can act as a trigger to encourage spawning.

ⓘ AVOID EXCESS FAT

Carnivorous species can be fed on items such as beef heart, but it is important to use only very lean meat. Otherwise the excess fat is likely to cause a nutritional imbalance, which may lessen the likelihood of successful breeding. Whereas beef heart can consist of as much as 50 percent fat on a dry matter basis, a commercial food typically has an equivalent figure of 5-8 percent.

Some fats such as beef are described as saturated, and these are not easy for fish to digest well. Much better for them are polyunsaturated fats in the form of items such as brine shrimps and krill. Carnivorous fish in particular need a source of these fats in their diet, allowing them to manufacture essential fatty acids. The terms "saturated and "polyunsaturated" when used to describe types of fat will be familiar to any human who has been on a diet! Just as the types of fat found in oily fish–the "polyunsaturated" variety–are recommended for us and the meat fats frowned upon, so for the aquarium occupant.

○ Various types of prepared food are now widely available, including freeze-dried live foods, flake and pellets.

These particular foods, the shrimps and krill—being a source of carotenoid pigments—also help to give fish their natural coloration. Such pigments are responsible for colors ranging from yellow through orange and red to green (the krib pictured below in its natural colors

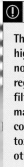

> ## ⓘ PROTEIN AND WATER POLLUTION
>
> The high nitrogenous content of protein means that uneaten high-protein foods will soon pollute the aquarium, so it is not a good idea to use high-protein items such as live foods regularly in a new aquarium. It is important to wait until the filter is functioning properly, especially where you are relying mainly on biological filtration, because high levels of protein could overload the system, causing a build-up of potentially toxic ammonia in the water. Frequent water changes will otherwise be necessary as a precaution.

is an example). Although artificial sources sometimes used for this purpose include plants such as marigold flowers and paprika.

The protein constituent of the diet is very important especially for young individuals, promoting healthy growth and recovery from injury. Protein is made up from amino acids, some of which must be present in the diet, because they cannot be manufactured in a fish's body. (Similarly humans cannot build all their required amino acids internally.) Most tropical fish foods contain at least 35 percent protein, whereas diets for young fish may have levels as high as 50 percent to meet their growth requirements.

⬅ Krib, or purple cichlid (*Pelvicachromis pulcher*). Like all the members of this genus usually found in the aquarium, such as the yellow krib (*P. humilis*) and eyespot krib (*P. subocellatus*) these fish are easy to please, accepting a wide variety of foods.

Vitamins and minerals

Vitamins are a diverse group of chemical compounds, which have specific roles within the body. Vitamin C is significant in helping the body to fight infections, while members of the vitamin B group play a key role in various metabolic reactions. Vitamins are divided into fat-soluble and water-soluble groupings; fat-soluble vitamins are stored in the liver. In total, approximately 14 different vitamins are believed to be important for fish. Formulated food is supplemented with these in the correct proportions, whereas the levels of the different vitamins in fresh foods vary.

Minerals and trace elements are also essential in the diet. Fish need only small amounts of these inorganic compounds—particularly trace elements—in order to ensure good health. Calcium, for example, helps the skeleton while iron is a vital constituent of the fish's blood, in the form of

> ### VITAMINS AND SHELF-LIFE
>
> Vitamins are one of the most perishable ingredients in fish food. It is therefore important to check on the recommended use-by date given on the packaging when buying a prepared fish food, because the vitamin content is only guaranteed for a certain period. It helps to buy reasonable (not bulk) amounts from a store with a high turnover so that you can use the food up, rather than having to discard it when the use-by date is reached.

hemoglobin. Although Rift Valley cichlids and other fish inhabiting hard waters can absorb some of the dissolved calcium, those native to soft-water regions (like tetras) need calcium supplements.

Finding food

The way in which fish locate and digest their food varies markedly between the different groups, often reflecting their environment. Those that live under fairly murky water conditions, such as various catfish, often have barbels, which are sensory organs located near the mouth. The barbels of nonpredatory species are much shorter than those that hunt, simply because they only need information from their immediate environment, rather than from a wider area.

Many fish, most notably the feared piranhas (*see* page 62, *Serrasalmus* spp.), have prominent and often very sharp teeth in their jaws to rip into their prey and tear off chunks of flesh. They can smell blood in the water. The teeth of the closely related black-finned pacu (*Colossoma macropomum*), in contrast, are less pointed, and more suited to crushing the vegetable matter on which these fish feed. They can detect fruits falling into the water, and congregate beneath such trees in the wild.

In some group of fish, the teeth may not be so obvious. Teeth located further back in the roof of the mouth in the region of the pharynx are described as pharyngeal teeth. These act rather as a grinding pad, breaking food down into smaller parts before it is swallowed. Many bottom-dwelling fish also ingest some of the substrate as they feed, and they may use this to grind up the food when chewing it on their pharyngeal teeth. Some fish have teeth in their jaws as well as pharyngeal teeth.

The transference of teeth away from the jawline has meant that the jaw shape of various fish has altered significantly. Some have evolved suckers that allow them to anchor on to rocks in fast-flowing streams. In other cases, the jaws themselves have developed as rasps. This has enabled fish to live without competing with each other in the same environment, and explains how there came to be so many African Rift Valley cichlid species.

Digestive structures

Carnivorous and herbivorous fish have a different lower digestive system. Predatory

⊕ Loricariid catfish like this bristle bushmouth (*Anicistrus ranunculus*) have suckermouths to stop themselves being swept away by strong currents, especially as they are not powerful swimmers.

fish typically have a digestive tract beginning with a large stomach where prey is stored, allowing the digestive process to start there. This can be seen in the case of the red-tailed catfish (*Phractocephalus hemioliopterus*), which grows to a large size, but is still popular with aquarists. Even in a young individual, a discernible swelling forms in the belly area just after the fish has fed.

Certain vegetarian characins, such as the lined citharinid (*Citharinus citharus*), have a muscular part to their stomach acting rather

FOOD STICKS

Food sticks are useful for larger fish, remaining buoyant for some time. It is important not to offer them to small fish because they will bite into them, splitting off small fragments. This will cause more wastage in the aquarium, which ultimately can add to the pollution. As in the case of pellets, always try to match these to the size of your fish.

like a bird's gizzard, grinding up the vegetable matter with the substrate that has been ingested. This helps to start the breakdown of the plant matter. The acids in the stomach of some tilapia cichlids are strong enough to dissolve the plant cell walls, releasing the nutrients within. Some fish, notably goldfish and other cyprinids, have no stomach at all. Instead, they have a slightly dilated area at the start of the small intestine where food enters after being swallowed and before passing directly into the intestinal tract.

Herbivorous fish have a much longer intestinal tract, because their source of nutrients is of relatively low nutritional value, and

⊙ Red-tailed catfish (*Phractocephalus hemioliopterus*). Their size means these are costly fish to house.

⬇ Some fish can be tamed sufficiently to take food from the hand. There is no room in a book like this to discuss the complex delights of koi keeping, but this pond fish by tradition is more and more kept in indoor aquariums as tank technology improves.

harder to digest. Rather like herbivorous mammals such as sheep, they rely on beneficial bacteria and other microbes in their digestive system to break down the cellulose in plant walls and gain access to the nutrients.

The most popular options

Today, you can buy a wide array of prepared foods containing all the key nutrients in the correct proportions. This choice is the result of extensive research, and has greatly simplified the task of ensuring the fish receive a balanced diet. In turn, this has enhanced the popularity of fish keeping, and contributed to breeding successes with many species.

Before deciding on which type of food to choose, however, it is important to consider the different properties of prepared diets and how these relate to the feeding habits of the fish themselves. It is no coincidence that flake foods are most widely used. As its name suggests, flake food has a very fine texture, and floats when dropped on to the water. It is useful for taming goldfish, for example, drawing these bottom-feeders up to the surface. In addition, surface-feeding fish, such as hatchetfish, will have plenty of time to nibble at the flakes before they become saturated and sink into the lower reaches of the water, where other fish such as tetras will seize morsels. Any remaining food will ultimately sink to the floor of the aquarium, to be eaten by catfish and other bottom dwellers along with any snails in the aquarium.

Some types of food pellet also float for some time, although the density of most pellets means they will sink straight to the floor of the aquarium. Floating pellets are ideal for larger goldfish, whether being housed in aquariums or ponds: the air trapped within the pellet provides buoyancy. These pellets provide the fish with a more concentrated form of nutrition than flakes.

Granules are another possible feeding option, but these sink quite rapidly and break down in the substrate, where they too will increase the burden on the filtration system. In contrast, pieces of flake here are more likely to be seen and eaten by the fish. It is important not to force bottom-dwelling fish to rely on leftover morsels: they should be provided with their own food. Sinking pellets are ideal for this purpose, but remember that it may not be a good idea to feed all the fish at the same time, because a number of the bottom-dwelling fish are more active at night than during the daytime, and this is the time when they need to be fed. Otherwise, food will be wasted.

Although there are special diets available for particular types of fish—especially the most popular species such as guppies—a typical flake food will suit most tropical fish. Certain dry foods have color-enhancing properties that can be useful, particularly for relatively young fish. Food such as peas, boiled lettuce, or spinach can be offered in limited quantities to fish requiring more vegetarian diets. A sliced ring of cucumber on the floor of the aquarium is often a favored food with catfish, and any left uneaten can be easily removed with a net. It is a good idea to stick to organic produce, because of the risk of pesticide residues that could be harmful to the fish.

Encouragement to feed

Many factors influence the appetite of fish. When transferred to new surroundings, fish may display very little interest in food for the first day or so, although bolder individuals may snatch at food as soon as it is offered. This is why it is important to keep a close watch on all the tank occupants, to ensure that they all have an opportunity to feed. Shy and nervous individuals often refuse food when housed in an aquarium without adequate cover. Try adding a clean, broken clay flowerpot on the substrate as a retreat for the fish, and then offer food at the entrance to its

STORAGE

The way in which fish foods are stored has a marked effect on their shelf life. They are sold in airtight containers, and need to be kept out of heat and light. Always be careful to keep an open tub well away from water too—even any condensation on the hood—because if any droplets fall into the container, then it will have to be discarded. These prepared foods will rapidly start to decompose if they become moistened, as this triggers both fungal and bacterial growth.

The food itself will remain fresh until it is opened, with most being packed today beneath an inner protective foil cap. This helps to prevent the oxygen in the air from causing a rapid deterioration in the vitamin level and the fat content as well.

The fact that a food contains all the necessary nutrients to keep a fish in good health does not mean that it can be encouraged to sample it, let alone eat it regularly. It can be particularly difficult to persuade carnivorous species to take inanimate prey, especially if their feeding habits are highly specialized. This often applies in the case of the elephant-nosed fish (*Gnathonemus petersii*), which uses its trunklike mouthparts to find worms and similar live foods on the bottom. With patience, however, you may be able to persuade these fish to switch across to deep-frozen foods.

In the case of this and similar "fussy" species, it is always worth asking about their diet before you buy the fish. For example, if they are on inanimate food, ask to see them being fed if possible. Be prepared to pay extra for fish that are clearly established in this way, because weaning them on to such foods can be a time-consuming and quite costly process.

As for bottom-feeding predatory species, movement of the substitute food is very important, if it is to be sampled. The currents coming from an internal power filter unit might provide this movement. Alternatively, you could offer food with blunt-ended forceps, encouraging the fish to strike at what it perceives to be live prey. When choosing such species at the outset, it is worth remembering that younger individuals can often be persuaded to take a substitute diet more easily than larger fish of the same species.

Predatory piranhas are illegal in some areas.

lair. This is often enough to persuade it to feed without any further problems. Altering the level of lighting in the aquarium can also be significant.

The way in which fish identify possible food items varies according to the species concerned. In the case of catfish such as Corydoras, the barbels close to their mouth are covered in external taste buds, enabling them to identify edible objects. The texture of the food can also be significant when it comes to encouraging fish to eat. Although it may seem strange in the case of freshwater fish, marine foods like krill are popular.

It is no coincidence that many fish foods are green, yellow, and red. These colors seem to be most appealing to fish, especially those living in clear water and possessing good color vision. You can condition fish in an aquarium to expect food after a time, as they will come to recognize the sound of you lifting the food chute or the flap on the lid of the aquarium.

Fresh and preserved foods

While prepared foods contain a balanced range of ingredients, fresh foods of various types nevertheless help to provide valuable variety in the fish's diet. Aquatic invertebrates such as Tubifex and Daphnia (water fleas) are commonly used for this purpose; brine shrimp (*Artemia*) are valuable for the rearing of young fry (*see* page 125).

Freeze-dried live foods of aquatic origins are safer and easier to store than fresh supplies. Midge larvae, known as bloodworms (*Chironomus*) because of their red coloration, can be supplied in this form, along with many other live foods. Freeze-drying has a number of advantages, not least that the food itself does not have to be kept in a freezer compartment. It can be fed to the fish straight from the container, without any need to defrost it beforehand. The process also kills off harmful organisms that could threaten the health of the aquarium occupants.

① SPITTING

It is not uncommon for predatory fish to strike at a possible item of food, and then spit it out again. Especially with recently acquired individuals, this may be an indication that they are sampling a food with which they are unfamiliar. Nevertheless, if this behavior continues and the fish's condition starts to deteriorate, the problem might be the bacterial infection often rather confusingly described as mouth "fungus" (*see* page 132).

① A magnified picture of bloodworm—a relatively safe and popular live food for a wide range of aquarium fish.

① DANGERS OF AQUATIC LIVE FOODS

There is a risk when using live foods of aquatic origins of introducing diseases into the aquarium. Tubifex worms, for example, often congregate in waters where there is a high organic content, close to sewage outlets for example. Cultures of daphnia may contain other harmful microbes as well as parasites.

Much depends on the origins of the creatures. It is actually possible to culture safe supplies of live food with little difficulty, such as mosquito or midge larvae, by leaving out a small container of water, where the insects will be attracted to lay their eggs. It is then simply a matter of removing the larvae once they hatch, with a small strainer, and transferring them to the aquarium.

Deep-frozen foods are popular too, being sold in small blister packs that can be defrosted easily. Typical examples include mussels and lancefish. Once they have thawed, pieces can be given to the fish, and very often prove more palatable than freeze-dried options. Other possibilities include shrimps sold for human consumption.

It is important to link the size of the live food to that of your fish. River shrimp, along with other live food such as crickets and waxmoth larvae, are better for larger carnivorous fish than whiteworm (Enchytraeus). These choices are widely available for reptiles.

How often to feed?

Most fish should be fed two or three times each day, to minimize wastage of food, which in turn will threaten to overload the filter. You can use feeding rings to prevent flake food being rapidly dispersed around the tank by the currents generated from a power filter. Although it is a matter of trial and error, the amount of food should be eaten within about five minutes. Watch the fish closely at this stage, simply because if any refuse to eat over the course of several days, this is likely to be a cause for concern.

Most fish keepers rely on a prepared food, augmented with fresh items or live food several times each week, to form the basic feeding regime for a community aquarium. If you are worried that nervous individuals may not be receiving an adequate share within a group, then you can offer a food block that attaches to the glass, so that you can watch them coming to feed there. Predatory fish, on the other hand, will not need feeding every day, especially as they grow older.

🔽 The use of a feeding ring will help to prevent food such as flake being dispersed by water currents around the aquarium.

TANK MONITORING

It is particularly important to monitor the water quality closely in a new aquarium. Unlike the situation in a river, there is no dilution of the waste matter here, and in the absence of a fully functional filter, chemicals can build up to toxic proportions, threatening the well-being of the fish. In the initial stages, there will be an accumulation of ammonia, followed by a slower rise in nitrite. This shows that the beneficial *Nitrosomonas* bacteria, which are responsible for undertaking this conversion, are starting to function effectively. Finally, there will be a detectable rise in nitrate, thanks to *Nitrobacter* bacteria, which utilize the dissolved nitrite.

Ammonia

The ammonia level needs to be as low as possible, because it is highly toxic to fish (*see* pages 29–32). It must be under 0.02 parts per million (ppm = mg/l). Measures such as adding zeolite to the aquarium will help to combat the ammonia problem in the early stages, as will the addition of seed cultures of bacteria over the longer term. When using a test kit, check whether it is reading just free ammonia (NH_3) or a combination of ammonia and less toxic ammonium (NH_4).

Nitrite poisoning should always be suspected if particular groups of fish in an aquarium die, while others that are known to have a

USING TEST KITS

These are widely sold in aquarist outlets, and are quite easy to use, although you might possibly encounter difficulties if you are color-blind. Always read the instructions, but in general terms, the following steps are necessary:

1. With a pipette kept for this purpose, take a sample of water from the aquarium, and transfer the required volume to the test tube.
2. Add the reagent, cap the tube, shake if necessary, and wait for the required time.
3. Stand or hold the tube alongside the color chart, which will allow you to determine the level of the chemical concerned, such as ammonia, in the water.

higher resistance survive. The nitrite level should not be allowed to rise above 0.2ppm, and if it appears to be increasing too rapidly in a new aquarium, then it is important to carry out a partial water change. This has the effect of diluting the remaining nitrite, making the aquarium safer for the fish.

The appearance of nitrates in solution is a sign that the aquarium is starting to mature. Having living plants in the aquarium will utilize this for their growth, preventing the level of nitrate from rising. Unfortunately, in the absence of such plants, algal contamination becomes more likely, simply because there is no competition for the dissolved nitrates in the water. Although nitrate is far less toxic to fish than either ammonia or nitrite, it is likely to lower their disease resistance, leaving them vulnerable to infection. Young fry, and discus of all ages are at greatest risk of being affected by nitrates in the water. In all cases, the nitrate level should be below 50ppm (mg/l).

You might want to use a reverse osmosis unit if nitrate levels are high in your drinking water. The unit attaches to a faucet and strains out the larger nitrate molecules, with pure water then passing through the membrane for use in the aquarium.

🔽 While only rarely used in the freshwater aquarium a nitrate filter offers an alternative (or a boost) to the usual biological filtration. It is especially useful where the local water supply has relatively high nitrate levels.

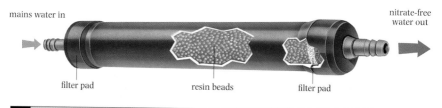

mains water in

nitrate-free water out

filter pad   resin beads   filter pad

NEED FOR WATER CHANGES

Any nitrate not utilized by plants as part of the Nitrogen Cycle will continue to accumulate in the aquarium. You may therefore have to carry out partial water changes more frequently if you have chosen plastic aquarium plants rather than living ones. Being relatively high in nitrates, this tank water can then be used to good effect for watering plants, serving as a fertilizer.

MAINTENANCE

There are thousands of different species of algae, and some will inevitably be present in the water. Other plants can also introduce them. So-called red algae often afflicts Cryptocornes, and can have adverse effects on them by colonizing leaf surfaces, while also progressing to spread more widely through the aquarium. The only solution to assist the recovery of individual plants is to cut off the affected leaves, in the hope that they will grow back successfully.

⬆ Algal growth can smother aquarium plants, even killing them.

Excessive lighting, appearing on the glass and also objects within the aquarium, will dramatically increase the risk of an algal explosion. Although some fish will browse on algae (see Chapter 3), it is not a good idea to allow this to build up, because excessive levels will not only appear unattractive but could possibly threaten the well-being of the fish by utilizing oxygen in the water after dark, when they are not photosynthesizing. Certain strains of algae also produce toxins that could harm the fish.

In the first instance, try reducing the length of time that the tank is illuminated, for example, or possibly checking the intensity of the lighting tubes. It is possible to remove the algal growth quite easily from the sides of the aquarium, by using one of the special scrapers that are available for this purpose. Long-handled designs can be used directly on the inner surface of the aquarium. Magnetic cleaners can be used through the panels of the tank. The scraper is held in place using a powerful magnet, allowing it to be drawn across the surface from outside the tank.

Always take care not to scratch the sides of an acrylic aquarium or to strip away the sealant of a glass tank. It can be harder to remove

There are algal-killing chemical solutions that can be used in the aquarium, and although these should not harm the fish when used as instructed, they may have a detrimental effect on the plants. The impact is unlikely to be immediately evident. Instead the effects only emerge later, often causing the leaves to become discolored.

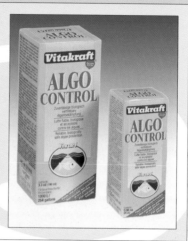

algal colonies elsewhere, within the airlift for example, or in tubing. This can be done by means of bottlebrushes of the appropriate size.

The plants will take time to become established in the aquarium, and a degree of dieback affecting the leaves is likely to be apparent at first. This can be minimized by ensuring the leaves are kept moist at all times and the plants themselves are always handled by their stems rather than the leaves. It is quite normal, however, for old leaves to die back as new ones grow, but discoloration of new growth in particular is likely to be a sign of problems.

Special general-purpose aquarium plant fertilizers are beneficial if they are used in accordance with the accompanying instructions. Beware of using just an iron fertilizer on its own, however, because it is likely to trigger a manganese deficiency. If you have a pet rabbit, you can bury one of the droppings in the substrate close to the plant's roots—this is regarded as a very effective fertilizer for aquatic plants.

Often, weak plant growth can indicate poor water quality. Cryptocornes, for example, typically die back when nitrate levels are high, while an excess of phosphate can result in leaves turning blackish. Poor growth can also be linked with inadequate lighting. Remember to replace fluorescent tubes within a year, because although their light output may not appear to have declined significantly, it will be less effective than before.

Problems can also sometimes arise when plant growth at the surface becomes luxuriant, to the extent that it masks off adequate light penetrating into the lower reaches of the aquarium, affecting the growth of plants there. In this case, simply thinning out the plants at the surface should prove adequate.

A deficiency of trace elements is a common cause of yellowing of the leaves. It is possible to distinguish between a deficiency caused by manganese, rather than iron, since in this case, the veins in the leaves remain green, whereas in cases of iron deficiency, the whole leaf is affected. *Vallisnerias* and *Echinodorus* are especially susceptible to problems of this type.

Filter management

Filter management itself in the early stages is quite straightforward. A sponge core, however, will need to be washed out every three weeks or so, to remove solid particles of debris which are accumulating in the core. These will otherwise reduce the flow of water through the filter and lessen its efficiency. This lessened efficiency depresses the available oxygen, threatening the survival of a beneficial population of bacteria here, and further compromises the efficiency of the filter as a result.

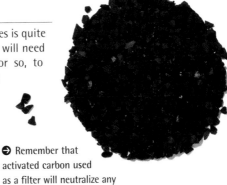

➲ Remember that activated carbon used as a filter will neutralize any medication in the water.

ⓘ DO NOT DESTROY

Although it is possible to purchase new cores for filters, this creates a difficulty because it means discarding the beneficial bacterial colony that has built up with it. Instead, it is better to wash out the foam filter medium. Do not run it under a faucet, however, because the chlorine in the water is also likely to harm the bacterial population. The best solution may be to squeeze and wring it out in some of the aquarium water removed when you are carrying out a partial water change. This will be sufficient to remove most of the debris and restore the efficacy of the filter. Alternatively, you can use dechlorinated water, which should be tipped away afterward rather than being used to replenish the tank. In some cases, you will have little choice other than to use a new core—monitor the water quality more frequently under these circumstances, although if there is also an adequate undergravel filter in operation, the effects should not be serious.

In the case of an undergravel filter, debris often builds up in the gravel filter bed, again reducing the efficiency of the filter. If uncorrected it can cause water quality deterioration. It is hence a good idea to use a gravel cleaner on a regular basis to freshen up the gravel when you carry out a partial water change. This simple device consists of a broad suction unit open at both ends, which connects to a length of plastic tubing, and works just like a siphon. When positioned at the level of the substrate, the suction currents created by the flow of water through the tubing cause the gravel to float around in the tube and displace accumulated debris. This is then drawn out in the water, while the pieces of gravel sink again. Move the gravel cleaner over as much of the floor as possible, being careful not to disturb plants; if any are displaced, they can be replaced. Take particular care of any young fry, to avoid them being sucked up into the bucket.

REMOVING WATER

When you need to carry out a water change, fill the length of tubing with dechlorinated water or water from the tank, and place a finger or thumb over both ends of the tube. Lower one end into the aquarium, releasing this finger first, before taking your finger off the other, which then allows water to flow into the bucket. NEVER be tempted to suck water through the tubing to start the siphoning process, as it could lead to health problems if you swallow any dirty water.

Water changes

When replenishing the water in the aquarium, always try to ensure that it is as close as possible to the temperature within the tank itself. It helps if you use a container of known volume, so you can easily calculate the amount of water conditioner that will be required. This must be added before the water is transferred to the aquarium.

It can be difficult pouring water into the tank directly from a bucket. Even if you do it slowly, it is likely to lead to quite powerful currents being set up in the tank. This could disturb the gravel and uproot the plants and it might also dislodge objects such as rockwork, with potentially serious consequences. There is also the risk that some of the water could be spilled on to surrounding furniture or carpeting if the bucket does not have a spout.

A better solution, therefore, may be a garden watering can. Never be tempted to use one that may have been used for garden chemicals, since any residue here will almost certainly prove harmful to the occupants of the aquarium. Remove the sprinkler and then slowly pour in the dechlorinated water, which should create a minimal current.

VACATION CARE

Fish are quite easy pets to care for when you are going on vacation, especially coldwater fish. Nevertheless, it is important to prepare in advance, to minimize the likelihood of any disasters in your absence. Start by carrying out a partial water change a couple of days before you go, along with filter maintenance as necessary. It is always useful to have a spare fluorescent light available, while a spare heaterstat may also be a useful investment.

Ensure there is adequate food too, if someone is going to feed the fish in your absence. This may not be necessary because there are slow-release weekend food blocks and larger vacation blocks available from specialist aquarist stores. These can simply be dropped in the tank and will not pollute the water. Another possibility to consider, especially for a short break, is to invest in an automatic feeder, which operates off a battery and will dispense a predetermined amount of food into the tank at a set time. Most adult fish,

⊙ A phosphate test kit. Levels of phosphates are increasing in some local water supplies, so it may be worth testing, particularly in the weeks following initial set-up, or if algae begin to get out of control.

assuming they have been eating regularly for some months, will actually not come to any harm if they are not fed for a week or two, particularly as they are likely to nibble at plant matter in the aquarium, although regular feeding is obviously preferable.

Even if you do not ask a friend to feed the fish, you should arrange for the tank—especially a tropical one—to be checked at least once a day in your absence. This will ensure that the heater is working properly, and also that none of the fish have died and triggered a rapid deterioration in water quality.

(!) OVERFEEDING

One of the major difficulties that you may face with a friend who has no experience of fish keeping is the risk that he or she will overfeed your fish while you are away. The consequences can be serious because the uneaten food builds up and pollutes the water. It may not be a bad thing to leave out the approximate quantity in a small pile so your friend can see the amount that is required.

MAINTENANCE SCHEDULES

DAILY CARE
On a daily basis, feed the fish, and check they appear healthy. If any are looking ill or have died, they should be removed. Check the water temperature from the thermometer reading, and that the filter and air supplies are working correctly.

WEEKLY CARE
Each week, particularly in the early stages before the natural balance is in the aquarium is established, carry out tests on the water for dissolved nitrogenous compounds, pH and softness. Keep the level of pollution as low as possible, with the use of a gravel cleaner. Carry out perhaps 10 percent water changes every week for the first two months or so.

MONTHLY CARE
Test the water chemistry each month, once the aquarium is established. Carry out more extensive water changes—perhaps 25 percent of the tank's volume—at this stage. Check the filter, clean the glass and gravel. Remove any plant leaves that are dying back.

ANNUAL CARE
More extensive cleaning is needed, with the tank being stripped down, and the fish removed. They can be kept in temporary accommodation while the gravel is scooped out and washed, along with ornaments. Keep some of the tank water however, to replenish the aquarium in due course—aquarists often describe this as "aged water." Divide plants, keeping healthy young growth for replanting. Check and change filter components as necessary. The air pump might benefit from a service, especially if it is proving noisy, and the airstones may need to be changed. Replace the fluorescent tubes, even if they are still working.

CHAPTER 5

Breeding

Some fish represent a greater challenge to breed successfully in a home aquarium than others, but many will reproduce quite readily. The likelihood of fry growing up successfully in a community aquarium is small, however, because they are likely to fall victim to tank occupants at an early stage in life—possibly even their own parents. As a result, you will usually need to invest in an additional tank and equipment for breeding purposes.

⬇ Many fish scatter their eggs at random but angels (*Ptero-phyllum* spp.) spawn on rocks or plants.

Some fish, notably members of the cichlid family such as the angelfish, may form a strong bond with each other, and once you have a compatible pair, they are likely to continue breeding repeatedly. There is more chance of success if the fish have grown up together—trying to introduce adult fish of this type together especially placing one in the tank of another, is likely to result in serious outbreaks of fighting, especially when they are in breeding condition.

BREEDING STRATEGIES

Fish can be broadly divided into two groups, based on their reproductive habits. Although most fish actually lay eggs, some, such as the guppy (*Poecilia reticulata*), produce live offspring, and they are known as livebearers. Their method of mating also differs from that of egg-layers. Livebearers display internal fertilization, whereas in the case of egg-layers, the process is much more haphazard. The male fish releases his sperm into the water as the female spawns nearby, in the hope

of fertilizing as many eggs as possible, although inevitably, some will drift on the currents and be missed.

In certain livebearers such as goodeids (Goodeidae), mating occurs as the result of sperm being passed directly from the cloacal opening of the male into that of the female. With guppies, platies, and other members of the Poeciliidae family, the anal fin of the male fish is modified into a thin tube, known as the gonopodium, through which sperm is transferred into the female's body. This ensures a much higher level of fertility.

Although the fry grow within the female's body, there is usually no actual placental connection to nourish them in the case of most livebearers, unlike the situation with mammals. The eggs are simply retained in the relative safety of the female's body and develop there up to the stage that the young are ready to emerge from their egg cases. This breeding method is described as ovoviviparous. Indeed, if you look closely when the female is producing her brood, you are likely to see the young fish being born in a curled-up state, just as they would lie in an egg.

The hazards of egg-laying

It is no coincidence that livebearers generally produce fewer offspring, typically 60-80, compared with the many hundreds of eggs usually laid by other fish. This is a reflection of the relative hazards of these means of reproduction. Simply scattering eggs at random means that most will fall victim to predators in the wild, with only a tiny proportion even surviving long enough to hatch into fry.

A few egg-laying species of fish do take particular care with their eggs. None is more dedicated than some of the cichlids living in the lakes of the Rift Valley in eastern Africa. In the case of these mouth-

↑ It is one of the most fascinating behavior traits of some adult cichlids to guard their offspring. A pair of rams (*Papiliochromis ramirezi*) is shown here with their young. The ram, or butterfly dwarf cichlid, is identified as *Microgeophagus ramirezi* by some authorities.

brooders, the female cichlid will scoop up the eggs into her mouth after the male has fertilized them. She then keeps them here, without feeding for approximately three weeks, until they have hatched. For a short time afterward, she will encourage the young fish to dart back to the safety of her mouth if danger threatens.

Other fish simply carefully choose where to lay their eggs and then try to guard them to ensure they hatch successful. The popular discus (*Symphysodon discus*) and angelfish (*Pterophyllum* spp.) should be provided with slate or clean clay flowerpots for this purpose, to encourage them to spawn in aquarium surroundings. They will then try to corral their fry once they hatch and look after them, with discus producing a special secretion on their flanks to nourish the offspring through the early stages of life.

BREEDING TRIGGERS

In the wild, fish commonly do not live in a constant environment. This in turn means they are more likely to breed at certain times of the year than others, based on the local water conditions. Nevertheless, having now been captive-bred for many generations, some species now prove to be more adaptable breeders than when they were first introduced to the hobby.

BREEDING TRIGGERS AND CONDITIONING

You will achieve the best breeding results by setting up special quarters for your fish, mimicking the conditions under which they breed in the wild. Moreover, conditions in a breeding tank can be manipulated as necessary. This advice applies especially in the case of egg-laying species, if only because their eggs are very vulnerable to being eaten almost immediately in aquarium surroundings.

First you must ensure that you have a pair of fish. Although visual sexing is quite straightforward in some species, it is virtually impossible in others, although generally, the bodies of female egg-layers will swell up as a result of their eggs just prior to laying, while male fish may become more colorful at this stage. Many fish will become mature between six and 12 months of age, although goldfish may not reach this stage until they are two years old.

Changing environmental conditions usually play their part in determining when fish will breed. Lighting can be especially significant in the case of fish such as goldfish, which originate from outside the tropics where day length is relatively constant. A slight increase in water temperature can also be significant for them.

● Sex tubercules on the gill cover of a male goldfish. These are only visible when these fish are in breeding condition.

On the other hand—in the Amazonian region, for example—water volume is often significant. There can be a change in water level of more than 50ft (15m) between river flows during the dry and wet seasons. Heavy rainfall stirs up the material in the water, filling up tributaries and flooding areas that for much of the year may be dry. These flooded areas of forest and more open country greatly expand both the range of the fish and their feeding opportunities, with mosquitoes and similar invertebrates multiplying rapidly in such areas of standing water.

By creating similar changes within the confines of a spawning tank, you should find that fish originating in these types of environments can be conditioned to start breeding successfully.

Modifying water conditions

Softer water conditions can trigger the breeding of Amazonian species such as various tetras and discus. This mimics the increase in rainfall that begins their breeding cycle in the wild, especially if combined with a slight drop of a degree or two in the water temperature as well, reflecting the increased flow of water.

The substrate may also need to be changed from gravel to peat, although you should only use special aquarium peat for this purpose. Start by simply filling the spawning tank with water and then tip the dry peat over the entire surface to a depth about 2in (5cm). It will take about a week for this to become saturated and sink to the bottom.

The water itself will take on a murky yellowish-brown hue, as the result of the tannins that have been introduced to it, along with beneficial trace elements. Fish keepers often describe this as black water, with its murky appearance matching that seen in waters such as the aptly named Rio Negro (Black River) in Brazil. Housing certain fish, particularly tetras, in this type of breeding setup will help to prevent damage to their eggs. Such species' eggs are photosensitive, and can be adversely affected by light.

Increasing the amount of live food in the fish's diet can also help to trigger the onset of breeding condition. This should start before they are moved to their spawning quarters. Whiteworms (*Enchytraeus*) are especially valuable for this purpose, and can be

ⓘ WATER SOFTENING EQUIPMENT

Reverse osmosis systems may be useful for water softening. Using rainwater itself for spawning tanks, especially in urban areas, can be risky because of the chemical pollutants that it is likely to contain.

BLACKWATER EXTRACT

One possibility when setting up a breeding tank for tetras, for example, is to use what is described as a blackwater extract, adding this to the aquarium water. It contains a distillation of key constituents such as peat extracts and trace elements found in this type of aquatic environment, and has similar effects on the water chemistry as peat itself.

cultured easily at home, from a starter culture sold by live food suppliers. You need to plan in advance, however, because it takes about a month for a colony to become productive.

Safeguarding the eggs

Many of the common aquarium fish, ranging from barbs to tetras, reproduce simply by scattering their eggs at random. Although these eggs may be adhesive, they are likely to fall to the floor of the aquarium and be eaten by the fish. It is therefore a good idea to include a spawning mop in the tank, where the female may be attracted to lay. This arrangement protects the eggs if they stick within the mop. The floor of the aquarium can be covered with a double layer of marbles, which will provide safety for the eggs falling there, as they will then be largely out of reach of the adult fish, passing down between the marbles.

The tank decor can also be important for egg-laying purposes. For example, species such as angelfish (*Pterophyllum* spp.) are likely to adopt pieces of slate firmly anchored in the substrate for egg laying. Since they care for their offspring, there is usually no need to move such fish to separate breeding quarters, but you may need to reassess the filtration arrangements for the early stages after the fry have hatched, opting for a sponge filter rather than a power filter over this period.

⊙ CURRENTS CAN BE DANGEROUS

The plants in a spawning tank play a crucial role in the breeding success of certain fish species. Members of the anabantoid family, for example, use their own mucus to build bubblenests at the water's surface. You should use floating plants as anchorage points in this case, while the filtration system needs to be very gentle so there is no risk of the nest being damaged by the current. In the wild, these fish naturally inhabit still stretches of water. Their tank should also be covered to protect against cold air currents, which can harm newly hatched fry. This advice also applies in the case of bubblenesting catfish.

The paradise fish male makes the bubblenest using mucus.

INDIVIDUAL REQUIREMENTS

In some cases in the wild, drying up of pools can act as a spawning trigger. The so-called annual killifish lay their eggs in the bottom of the muddy pools that they inhabit. As the water continues to evaporate, drying out these hollows and suffocating the fish, so the mud itself dries out, forming a protective crust over the eggs buried there. Then once the rains return, the shallow pools come back to life. The fry hatch and feed on the insects breeding there.

In aquarium surroundings, simply lowering the water level in the spawning tank will provide the stimulus for these beautiful small fish to start breeding. You can then transfer the adult fish back to their regular housing, allowing the tank to dry out, before flooding the base again in due course to stimulate the hatching process.

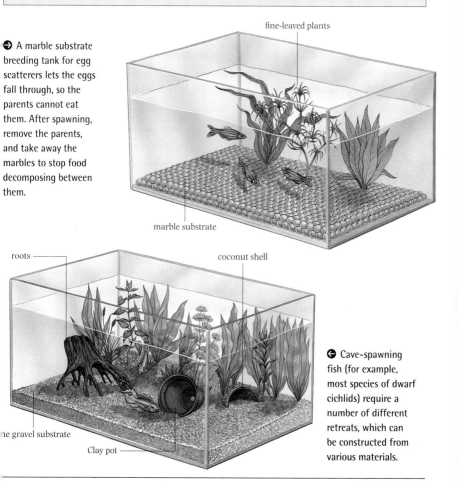

➲ A marble substrate breeding tank for egg scatterers lets the eggs fall through, so the parents cannot eat them. After spawning, remove the parents, and take away the marbles to stop food decomposing between them.

fine-leaved plants

marble substrate

roots

coconut shell

ne gravel substrate

Clay pot

⬅ Cave-spawning fish (for example, most species of dwarf cichlids) require a number of different retreats, which can be constructed from various materials.

Those cichlids that normally spawn in underwater caves can usually be persuaded to do so, when provided with a clay flowerpot partially submerged in the substrate.

Setting up a spawning tank

Set up the spawning tank several days in advance. It is better to use an external panel heater in this case, so there will be no risk of eggs or indeed young fry being adversely affected by it, under the control of an internal thermostat. It is generally a good idea to keep the decor to a minimum, and set up a sponge filter, which has already been seeded using some water from the main aquarium. This will provide gentle yet effective biological and mechanical filtration.

For cyprinids, it may be a good idea to transfer the female with two males. This can stimulate the female to spawn more effectively. It can help if the fish have been housed and conditioned separately, although this also is not strictly essential.

Egg laying is most likely to occur in the morning, especially if a few rays of sun land on the sides of the tank. Transfer the fish overnight therefore, and move them back to the aquarium once spawning has been completed, except in the case of male anabantoids, who will guard their bubblenest until their fry hatch.

Eggs are even more vulnerable to predators than fry, which can take evasive action as they grow older. Hatching is therefore often a relatively short process, with the young fish emerging within 48 hours of egg laying, depending on the species. The fry are not free-swimming at this stage; instead they rest on the floor of the aquarium. They rely on their yolk sacs to nourish them. These yellowish swellings on the underside of the body are absorbed within a few days, after which you will see the young fish starting to swim around the spawning tank seeking their own food. They begin to feed on tiny microscopic particles.

Some fish keepers rely on cultures of infusoria to meet the needs of their young fish. It is very easy to set up a culture simply by adding some hay to a clean jar of water and leaving it to stand in the sun. Once it starts to turn cloudy, infusoria have developed. You can then provide small amounts for the young fish using a pipette, through the day. Alternatively, you can just add formulated fry foods to the tank. It is important to choose the right type of food, however. Anabantoid fry, for example, have relatively small mouths

◑ The fry of the paradise fish (*Macropodus opercularis*) in the bubblenest are 24 hours old. Any that fall out are replaced. The gouramis are the most famous nest builders, along with their close relatives, the *Colisa, Trichogaster, Trichopsis, Belontia* and *Pseudosphromenus* genera. But even some catfish, such as *Hoplosternum*, build bubblenests.

and so require correspondingly small particles of food. Otherwise, they will starve.

You can offer brine shrimp (*Artemia*) larvae, often known as nauplii, as food as young fish grow larger. These are usually purchased in the form of eggs, which need to be kept in a sealed container to avoid attracting moisture from the atmosphere. Moisture as well as heat will seriously affect the numbers that hatch, so it can actually make economic sense to buy the eggs in relatively small quantities.

You can buy special hatching kits for the eggs, but you can carry this out quite easily in a small tank at home, keeping the water heated to 75°F (24°C). In addition to the brine shrimp eggs, you also need to buy some special marine salt, and an air line running off an air pump (*see* box right).

Another possibility to consider as a food for young fish is microworms. These are sold in starter cultures and can be bred in a similar way to whiteworm. A useful stand-by in an emergency is hard-boiled egg yolk. Cook and allow to cool thoroughly, before removing the yolk and squeezing this through muslin to provide the young fish with fine particles of this high-protein food. Beware, though, because egg yolk will pollute the water readily, so you should only offer small amounts at any stage.

HATCHING NAUPLII
1. Mix the marine salt thoroughly with the water so it dissolves.
2. Add the required quantity of eggs, and switch on the air pump with the bubbles produced through the airline serving to keep the eggs in motion.
3. Hatching of the nauplii will take about 36 hours, with the indigestible shells rising to the surface.
4. Sieve these out first, and discard them. Then remove the brine shrimp nauplii as required.
5. Dip these in some dechlorinated freshwater, to rinse them, before offering them to the fry.

BREEDING LIVEBEARERS

It is possible to rear some fry in a tank with other livebearers, but many of the young fish are likely to be eaten by other occupants of the tank. Stepping up the number of feeds in the crucial early days may help to save some of them. There is the risk that the water conditions will deteriorate more rapidly. You can also safeguard young livebearers with dense planting, providing them with plenty of

◑ The fry of livebearers are at risk of being eaten by their mother and other adult fish.

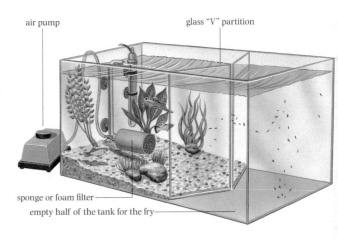

⊃ Tank set-up for livebearers with a "V"-shaped insert that has a gap to let the fry swim through. You can also split the tank with a wide mesh or perforated divider.

air pump

glass "V" partition

sponge or foam filter

empty half of the tank for the fry

hiding places close to the floor of the aquarium. Try using plants such as Java moss (*Vesicularia dubyana*) for this purpose.

You can achieve the greatest success, however, by transferring a gravid female to a separate tank before she gives birth. It is important to move the female at a relatively early stage; otherwise, she may give birth to her offspring prematurely, and they will fail to survive. It is usually possible to determine when a female is becoming gravid by the swollen abdomen. Eventually, she develops a dark spot on her flank just before giving birth, although by this stage, it will be risky to move her as she could easily abort her offspring.

The many different designs of breeding trap on the market all have the same function—to protect the young fish from their mother. She remains confined within the trap while her offspring can escape through small slits or similar spaces into the safety of the tank itself.

Once the female has produced her brood, she will need to be put back in the main aquarium, so her young can be reared safely on their own. They can then be introduced to the aquarium in due course, when they are larger. The length of time between broods varies, depending partly on the temperature of the water, but guppies for example carry their young for about four weeks.

⊙ SIZE ISN'T EVERYTHING

When seeking breeding stock, especially with guppies, it is helpful to choose the largest females because they are likely to produce the largest number of offspring. Unfortunately, even though you may choose the most attractive males in the tank to pair at home with the females, they will almost certainly not sire any of her subsequent progeny. This is because female guppies only need to mate once to produce broods throughout their lives.

Growing on

Young fish are introduced to other foods as they start to grow. Flaked food, for example, can be powdered very easily through your fingers, and granules will break down quite readily in water. You need to be prepared to space out the young fish as they grow, which may entail transferring some to another aquarium. Overcrowding is not only likely to stunt their growth—it could even affect their survival. The risk of rapidly deteriorating water conditions rises significantly as the appetites of the fish increase and their waste output grows correspondingly, in the face of a restricted filter system.

It will help significantly if you have a large, established tank with a suitable filtration system where the young fish can be grown on. Keep a watch on the group as they grow. There may be the occasional individual that is deformed in some way, either missing an eye or possibly having difficulty in swimming. It is better for these fish to be killed painlessly if they are severely handicapped.

When faced with a large brood of fish, ask your local aquatic stores if they would be interested in taking the surplus stock. Many are often keen to obtain locally bred fish, although do not expect to get rich on this basis!

⊙ A floating breeding trap in use. Breeding traps allow young livebearers to escape from their mother by dropping into the box body below.

CHAPTER 6

Keeping Fish Healthy

You are most likely to encounter health problems in the early weeks after setting up the aquarium, partly because the water conditions will be less than ideal at this stage. The fish themselves will also be faced with the stress of adapting to new conditions, and so are more vulnerable to illness as a consequence.

➊ Emaciation can indicate piscine tuberculosis or, in this case, neon tetra disease.

It is especially important to watch them closely at this stage, so as to be able to detect any obvious signs of illness. By acting fast, you should be able to prevent any epidemic of disease that could threaten all the aquarium occupants. You will also be aiding the recovery of individual fish that do fall ill.

SIGNS OF ILLNESS

Always try to locate all the fish when feeding them. This will be easier with those such

---

① AT AN ANGLE

The way in which fish swim can betray a health problem. Fancy goldfish with corpulent bodies, such as moors or pearlscales, may start swimming at an abnormal angle in the water. Mild cases could be the result of indigestion, so try a high-roughage diet, offering defrosted frozen peas for example. Often though, the cause is a distortion of the swimbladder, which serves to control the fish's buoyancy. It can be a developmental abnormality, which becomes worse as the fish grows larger. This is a difficult problem to overcome, although lowering the water level for a time may help, as can increasing the water temperature slightly, especially if the room is relatively cold.

➜ A change in the fish's swimming pattern often indicates illness. This fish has a swimbladder malfunction.

as tetras, which swim in the midwater areas, rather than with catfish, loaches, or other fish that either hide away or feed at night. Some symptoms are common to various illnesses, so recognizing signs of ill health in fish may be reasonably straightforward. It might be harder, though, to identify the cause of the problem with certainty.

Abnormal swimming patterns can also be a sign of old age. In the case of livebearers, it is often a sign of senility. On the other hand, fish that swim repeatedly against rocks are likely to be suffering from external parasites, and are trying to relieve the irritation on their bodies in this way.

Swimming difficulties can sometimes be linked with fin problems. Clamped fins, held closed, may indicate poor general ill health, whereas damaged fins can be indicative of deterioration in water quality or bullying. Some fish, such as tiger barbs (*Barbus tetrazona*), are well known as fin-nippers, and companions with long, flowing fins are most likely to fall victim to them.

Fin damage can heal effectively, but recurrent injuries are likely to predispose to opportunistic fungal infections. Weakened individuals should be transferred to a hospital tank where they can recover alone. There is likely to be no long-term solution to the problem of fin nipping, other than to separate the fish permanently. Fin nipping tends not to happen in the wild, because the fish are not living in such close quarters, but repeated assaults of this type are likely in the aquarium.

DROPSY

Dropsy is not a disease but a symptom. It is a buildup of fluid inside the body cavities or within the tissues. There can be various underlying causes, including gill and kidney bacterial or parasitic infections, or liver disfunction. By the time a fish shows signs of dropsy it is very ill and may be a breeding ground for infection that threatens its tankmates. If you cannot quarantine, euthanasia may be the kindest option.

SETTING UP A HOSPITAL TANK

A relatively small tank will suffice for sick fish. The floor should be left bare, with filtration being provided by a simple sponge filter, rather than a design that has carbon at its core. This is because many of the medications used to treat fish ailments will be deactivated if they are filtered through carbon. It helps to set the thermostat 2–4°F (1–2°C) higher than normal: raising the water temperature stimulates the fish's immune response, helping it to fight infection more effectively. Keep the decor in the tank to a minimum, and use plastic plants because they can be disinfected easily. A clay flowerpot on its side can provide a retreat for more nervous species. By lessening the stress on a sick fish, you can increase the likelihood of recovery.

The only serious disease directly associated with aquarium fish that can be transferred to people is piscine tuberculosis. Unfortunately, the signs are not diagnostic, although affected fish appear to be in poor general health. They do not feed and will lose weight, with their coloration fading as well. By wearing disposable gloves, you will be protecting yourself against this infection. They prevent the mycobacteria responsible for the infection (which are different from those causing human tuberculosis) from entering your body through any cuts or grazes on your hands. Piscine tuberculosis causes a human skin infection called a granuloma, which will require prolonged treatment with antibiotics. It is not usually possible to treat sick fish successfully, however, and the tank will need to be stripped down, disinfected and refilled before restocking.

A CLOSED SYSTEM

The aquarium is a closed circulatory system, so that any harmful microbes in the water will probably multiply, increasing in numbers until they can overcome the body defenses of the fish. Aquarium fish are actually at greater risk of succumbing to illness compared with their wild relatives, simply because they are living at higher densities in a closed setup. Fresh water is only added to the aquarium when water changes are carried out, and not continuously by natural flow. This means that the accumulation of nitrites, for example, is also likely to be much higher than fish would face in the wild.

TREATMENTS

Medication based on various dyes, such as malachite green, have long been used for treating fish ailments, but as with all treatments, they must be used strictly in accordance with the accompanying dosage instructions. Otherwise they can prove toxic. It is particularly important not to mix remedies—for example, if you have a fish suffering from both a parasitic ailment and an accompanying fungal infection—unless you are certain they can be used safely in combination.

❯ One remarkable self-defense mechanism of some fish that are prone to infection by skin parasites, like these pencilfish, is the secretion of guanine, a substance found in the liver and pancreas of many animals, onto the exterior of the body.

Aside from restricting the spread of infection, a hospital tank stops any harmful side effects of these treatments from entering the main aquarium. They will often discolor the water, but more significantly, they are likely to compromise the effectiveness of beneficial bacteria in the filtration system. They could also end up being prematurely deactivated in the filter. There is the further likelihood that they will stain the aquarium sealant, permanently discoloring it, which is why an acrylic tank is usually preferable for housing sick fish.

Natural remedy

Specific natural treatments are now available for treating aquarium fish. Many of these treatments, based on tea tree (*Melaleuca*) extracts, have proved very successful in treating fin damage and similar wounds, helping to guard against bacterial diseases. The Aboriginal people of Australia first identified tea tree itself as a plant that protected against infections.

Bacterial illnesses

Antibiotics can be useful in treating bacterial ailments in fish, although these drugs are only available on veterinary prescription in a number of countries. Antibiotics may be used in various ways. Sometimes, they may be administered directly to a sick fish, particularly larger and more valuable individuals, by means of an injection. Medicated foods are not commonly used for the treatment of fish in home aquariums, although they can be useful in combating illness within a group, provided that the fish are still eating.

Where there is a superficial infection, then it is usually best to place the fish temporarily in an antibiotic bath. This must be covered so that the fish will not be able to leap out of the container while it

◔ A very severe case of fin rot affecting an angelfish (*Ptero-phyllum scalare*). Early treatment greatly improves the likelihood of recovery.

Poor water conditions and injury together play a major part in the spread of piscine disease. Fish that have suffered from scale damage and lost some scales are especially vulnerable. Bacteria can then invade the underlying tissue, causing ulceration that results in a cavity developing here. At this point, opportunistic fungi in the water are likely to invade the wound, resulting in a secondary fungal infection. This causes whitish areas, indicative of probably fatal fungal growth, to develop.

If transferred without delay to a hospital tank, however, an affected fish has more chance of recovery. Under these circumstances, there will be a much lower concentration of fungal organisms in the water. These can be present in quite large concentrations in established aquariums, but typically cause no harm, only becoming apparent following an injury, or when an individual fish is already weakened for another reason.

There can be confusion between bacterial and fungal ailments. For example, the disease known as mouth fungus (*right*) is actually caused by *Flexibacter* bacteria. The behavior of affected fish changes as a result of this infection, as they may be seen shimmying in the water, with their bodies moving from side to side, while they also lose their appetites, spitting out food.

Fungal infections usually cause white streaks that create a halo–like effect on the side of the fish, or sometimes a denser appearance like cotton wool. Direct treatment of the affected area should help to overcome infections of this type, with a small, clean paintbrush often being useful for this purpose. This can speed up the healing process, as well as curbing the growth of the fungus, which can spread at an alarming rate.

is being treated. The strength of the solution and the length of time that the fish is kept here are important considerations, just as with proprietary remedies. Repeated treatment in this way is likely to be necessary, to overcome the infection.

In the case of ulcers on the body resulting from bacterial infections, then applying an antibiotic directly to the wound can be more effective and less stressful. The fish will need to be lifted out from its tank in a net, with the medication being applied carefully on a cotton bud saturated with the solution, to the site of the injury. Just as when giving the fish a bath, only dechlorinated water should be used to make

An ulcer often results from initial scale damage, with the affected area becoming infected by bacteria in the water.

up any antibiotic solution. Obviously, prepare everything first so the fish can be transferred straight back to the tank after being treated, so that it is kept out of water for as short a time as possible.

VIRAL INFECTIONS

Viral ailments are not especially common among aquarium fish. Any illnesses of this type tend to be more host-specific than problems such as fungal infections. Goldfish (*Carassius auratus*), for example, can be at risk from spring viraemia of carp (SVC), a serious disease with symptoms including hemorrhaging and dropsy. Another source of illness is carp pox, caused by a herpes virus that strikes when fish are weakened or stressed, and leading to white waxy swellings over the body.

Recent research does suggest viruses may be more of a threat than previously thought. A case in point is the discovery of Singapore angel disease, caused by a virus that has been identified in the part of Asia where angelfish (*Pterophyllum* spp.) are bred commercially. As with many viral infections, mortality during an outbreak is high, and the problem is likely to become apparent before the fish reach the home aquarium.

⚠ FUNGUS AND FISH EGGS

Sometimes a number of fish eggs start to develop fungus. Under normal circumstances, only infertile eggs develop fungus, but there can be a possible problem if they form the majority of those laid, particularly where they have been allowed to fall down between marbles where they will be hard to remove. This pollutes the water, just as the young fry are starting to hatch.

It may therefore be a good idea to remove the marbles from the spawning tank once you have taken out the adult fish, so that any large batches of infertile eggs can be removed easily. Some fish, such as bumblebee gobies (*Brachygobias xanthozona*), appear to be more vulnerable to this particular problem than others. You need to take particular care if treating eggs or young fry, because those remedies containing copper in particular are likely to be harmful, causing developmental abnormalities.

The lymphocystis virus is more benign, but it can affect a variety of fish. A particularly high incidence has been recorded in glassfish (*Chanda ranga*) that have been injected with colored dyes to create striking colors in the muscles of their essentially transparent bodies. It is thought that transmission of the virus is linked to the injection process, since ordinary glassfish do not seem so susceptible to the infection. This welfare consideration is another reason why trade in dyed fish should be discouraged.

The lymphocystis virus causes small, tumor-like swellings over the body. They can increase in size and become quite disfiguring, although they are not highly infectious. They are not normally fatal either, although occasionally, similar growths develop inside the body, where they can have serious effects on the functioning of the body organs.

PARASITES

In contrast to vial infections, many parasitic ones can be spread very easily within the confines of the aquarium. One such fast-spreading infection is the illness popularly known as white spot, because of the associated signs. Its slightly more scientific name is "ich" thanks to the name of the unicellular microbe (*Ichthyophthirius multifiliis*) that is responsible for this condition.

Unfortunately, once the signs of white spot appear it is likely that these parasites will be widely distributed in the aquarium, since only this part of the lifecycle is visible to the naked eye. The infection is commonly introduced in water with new fish, from a

! THE TOMITE TIMEBOMB

The free-living stage in the white spot lifecycle is called a tomite, with potentially as many as 1,000 tomites being released from every white spot on the fish's body. This is what makes the infection so devastating within the confines of an aquarium. In the wild, many of the tomites would die before they come into contact with a host, which they must do within approximately 24 hours of hatching. In an aquarium, however, they can build up to almost plague proportions, so that all the fish will be exposed to large numbers of them.

◑ White spot is a serious parasitic ailment that spreads quickly, even just through the introduction of contaminated aquarium water. It is the most common disease in the fresh-water aquarium.

contaminated tank, emphasizing the importance of quarantining any new fish that you buy to add to an established aquarium. It is much easier to prevent infections from gaining access at this stage rather than eliminating them later.

When it comes into contact with a fish, the tomite embeds itself into the body, being transformed into what is called a trophozoite, which will in turn give rise to the visible white spot. As they rupture releasing the tomites, the scars created by the trophozoites leave the fish's body at risk from attack by both fungi and bacteria. If left untreated, mortality among the fish in an aquarium will be high, following sequential attacks by tomites that will progressively weaken them. Treatments are directed against killing off the tomites in the water, while carrying out a partial water change should lessen their numbers here too. If you have more than one aquarium, take particular care when netting fish, because these parasites can easily be transferred in this fashion, through water droplets.

Another microscopic parasite that can cause health problems—particularly in the case of labyrinth fish (Anabantidae) and danios

PLANT AND ANIMAL

Oodinium is an unusual organism in that it contains chlorophyll, like plants, and can photosynthesize under suitable conditions. It is also a successful parasite and will breed on the sides of fish. Every *Oodinium* parasite can give rise to 200 spores, which will again multiply very rapidly in an aquarium. As an adjunct to treatment, simply raising the water temperature slightly will shorten the time down to a day within which these spores need to find another host. Otherwise, this interval can be up to five times as long, leaving the fish at greater risk of becoming infected as a result.

(*Danio* spp.)—is *Oodinium*, the cause of so-called velvet disease. These parasites again attack the fish's body, creating a shiny yellowish-gray hue on the surface. Affected individuals will often rub themselves against decor in the tank in an attempt to soothe the resulting irritation.

Some individual species of fish are more vulnerable to certain types of parasite than others. In the case of discus (*Symphysodon aequifasciata*), the protozoa known as *Hexamita* is involved in the development of so-called "hole in the head" disease. This problem first manifests itself in the guise of pale areas on the head, which open up to form ulcerated areas. Although sometimes present in the digestive tract of these fish (where it causes no harm), *Hexamita* will attack weak individuals, or those that are under stress. Use a food containing vitamin C to combat the stress and add green stuff to the diet to help to prevent this problem. If it has developed, it requires rapid veterinary treatment with metridazole-based drugs to minimize the risk of permanent scarring.

Not all parasitic ailments can be treated easily, as in the case of so-called neon tetra disease, which is most commonly encountered in these particular fish, but has been documented in a number of other species too. It is caused by a parasite known as *Pleistophora hyphessobryconis*. Loss of body coloration is a clear sign of this infection, with the red on the sides of neon tetras (*Paracheirodon innesi*) becoming significantly paler than normal. Introducing a sick individual into the aquarium will soon result in the spores being released and threatening the other fish here.

There are other, larger parasites that may occasionally attack fish, particularly goldfish (*Carassius auratus*). These include anchor worms (*Lernaea*), which look like threads of cotton hanging off the sides of

🔼 Environmental problems may predispose discus to hole-in-the-head disease.

🔽 Anchor worms attach to the sides of the fish, but can be treated quite easily.

the fish. Argulus or fish louse (although it is actually a crustacean, related to crabs) can also be a problem in fish that have been reared in ponds, although their relatively large size means that they are easily spotted when the fish are caught up and transferred to aquarium surroundings. The bites of fish lice can trigger infections, but medical treatment will kill these parasites effectively.

Internal parasites are far less of a problem in fish, because they do not spread so easily through the water. Infections of this type are much harder to identify and treat successfully, however. This is partly because the clinical signs are less clearly defined. A fish suffering from intestinal worms is likely to develop a swollen abdomen, for example, which in turn affects its ability to swim. This could be linked with a number of other complaints however, effectively causing dropsy.

Parasitic flukes have a flat-bodied shape. They usually spread through intermediate hosts, with aquatic snails often featuring in their life cycles. Unfortunately, flukes often display a more aggressive manner of spread than intestinal worms, becoming free-swimming when they leave the snail's body and directly attacking any fish in their vicinity. Eye flukes will cause a change in the appearance of the eye, often resulting in it becoming cloudy. Treatment in this case is not really possible, although these parasites are very rare in aquarium fish.

EMERGENCIES

It is surprisingly easy to poison fish inadvertently these days by using household chemicals near the aquarium. Always be sure to read the labeling carefully when using aerosols of any kind: they can be wafted on air currents and drawn into the tank through the air pump. Even tobacco smoke has been shown to be harmful to guppies (*Poecilia*

SOME GOOD NEWS

The complex life cycle of many of these internal parasites also means that epidemics of disease with resulting widespread mortality are not common among aquarium fish. In the case of tapeworm infestations as an example, the end host of the tapeworm is usually a fish-eating bird. The tapeworm eggs therefore pass out in its droppings, and may be eaten by small crustaceans, with the initial development of the tapeworm occurring in their bodies. The fish then eats the crustacean and becomes infected in due course, being described as an intermediate host. This is because the life cycle of the tapeworm can only be completed when a bird eats the fish itself. It is therefore clear that the risk of aquarium fish acquiring this type of parasite is highly unlikely, although it is possible an individual could acquire a tapeworm infestation from *Daphnia* (water fleas) collected from a pond, rather than being cultured at home.

ⓘ CONSTIPATION

White-trailing lengths hanging out of the fish's anus will sometimes be visual evidence of intestinal worms. Far more common, however, can be trails of darker fecal material, especially in goldfish, which are indicative of constipation. This is most like to arise on a diet comprised entirely of flake food. Varying the diet should overcome this problem quickly.

reticulata), while you need to take particular care if you are using insecticides of any kind, whether for household plants, as bug killers, or flea control products for use on carpeting.

The signs of poisoning depend partly on the chemical involved, but usually, all the fish will be seen in distress and dying, in a relatively short interval after the treatment was used. It might even be following a partial water change, if you forgot to add the water conditioner to neutralize chlorine or chloramine present here. There is also a possibility that your water company may have added a pesticide product through the mains to sanitize the water, although this type of measure is usually announced in advance.

You need to take emergency action to save as many fish as possible under these circumstances, by catching them up and transferring them elsewhere in a clean container filled with dechlorinated water. It will then be a matter of stripping out the aquarium, and placing the fish back here as soon as the water is safe again.

POWER CUTS

Another utility problem that can arise is a loss of power. In the case of coldwater fish, this is unlikely to cause any major problems, although the activity of a biological filter will be depressed. The situation can be more serious with tropical fish however, because the heating will be affected along with the filtration and lighting systems. In the short term, this should not cause serious problems, and you can seek to conserve the heat of the water by covering the tank with a blanket or quilt after switching off the lighting to guard against the risk of fire if the power comes back on in your absence. Do not lift off the hood, as this will result in a loss of heat. You can monitor the water temperature with the thermometer.

If it appears that it could be a long shutdown, there is nothing to be gained by heating water to add directly to the aquarium. This is likely to have a detrimental effect on the water hardness, as the heating process removes the temporary hardness from the water. It is much better simply to fill a hot water bottle instead, and leave this to float in the aquarium, having baled out some tank water first to prevent any overflow.

When the heat comes back on, allow the water to warm up gradually—again, this will be far less traumatic for the fish. Only once it is back to its normal temperature should you replace water that may have been removed. A short loss of power is unlikely to have any long-term effects on most aquarium fish—their metabolisms tend to react by shutting down—but you should be particularly alert for signs of any fungal infections that may develop over the course of the next few days.

Further Reading

Alderton, David, *The International Encyclopedia of Tropical Freshwater Fish* (Howell Book House, New York, USA, 1997).

Alderton, David, *The Complete Guide to Fish Care* (Mitchell Beazley, London, UK, 1998).

Alderton, David, *Cichlids: Know Your Angelfish, Oscars, Discus and Others* (BowTie Press, California, USA, 2002).

Andrews, Chris, *A Fishkeeper's Guide to Fish Breeding* (Salamander Books, London, UK, 1986).

Andrews, C., Excell, A., and Carrington, N., *The Manual of Fish Health* (Salamander Books, London, UK, 1988).

Baensch, Hans A., and Riehl, Rudiger, *Aquarium Atlas Vols 1–3*, (Baensch, Melle, Germany, 1987, 1993, 1996).

Banister, K., and Campbell, A. (eds.), *The Encyclopedia of Aquatic Life* (Facts on File Inc., New York, USA, 1985, 1998).

Burgess, Warren E., *Colored Atlas of Miniature Catfish: Every Species of Corydoras, Brochis and Aspidoras* (TFH Publications, Neptune, USA, 1992).

Dawes, John, *Complete Encyclopedia of the Freshwater Aquarium* (Firefly, Ontario, Canada, 2001).

Hieronimus, Harro, *Guppies, Mollies, Platys—A Complete Pet Owner's Manual* (Barron's, New York, USA, 1993).

Hiscock, Peter, *Creating a Natural Aquarium* (Interpet, Dorking, UK, 2000).

Jepson, Lance, *A Practical Guide to Keeping Healthy Fish in a Stable Environment* (Interpet, Dorking, UK, 2001).

Lambert, Derek, *A Practical Guide to Breeding Your Freshwater Fish* (Interpet, Dorking, UK, 2001).

Pinter, Helmut, *Labyrinth Fish* (Barron's, New York, USA, 1986).

Sandford, Gina, *The Questions and Answers Manual of the Tropical Freshwater Aquarium* (Andromeda Oxford, Abingdon, UK, 1998).

Scheurmann, Ines, *Aquarium Plants Manual* (Barron's, New York, USA, 1993).

Smartt, J., and Blundell, J.H., *Goldfish Breeding and Genetics* (TFH Publications, Neptune, USA, 1996).

Tekriwal, K.L., and Rao, A.A., *Ornamental Aquarium Fish of India* (Kingdom Books, Waterlooville, UK, 1999).

Websites

Probably the biggest aquarium website. Includes beginner information in Basic Resources: http://www.aqualink.com

General tropical fish site links: http://www.suite101.com/linkcategory.cfm/14243/24419

The Tropical Tank—fish and aquarium-related links: http://www.thetropicaltank.co.uk/links.htm

This is only a single page! But it does have an interesting point to make if you are impatient to get started with stocking your aquarium: http://tomgriffin.com/aquamag/cycling.html

A German website, but English is "spoken". Individual species given full coverage, including new entries to the trade, along with photographs: www.aquarium-dietzenbach.de

Glossary

Acidic A reading on the **pH** scale below 7.0.

Adipose fin A smaller fin which is sometimes present along the back, located between the **dorsal fin** and the **caudal fin.**

Adsorb The way in which molecules may adhere to a porous surface such as carbon, which can help to filter out unwanted substances in aquarium water.

Algae Microscopic plants present in water, which can coat glass, rockwork and other surfaces in the aquarium, especially under high light intensity.

Alkaline A reading on the **pH** scale above 7.0.

Anal fin Unpaired fin in front of the vent, which may be modified into a **gonopodium.**

Barbels Fleshy filaments around the mouth that have a sensory function. Most common in fish inhabiting murky waters, especially catfish.

Biotope The fish and its natural environment.

Blackwater extract Commercially available preparations that mimic the soft, acidic water conditions prevalent in the Amazonian region and elsewhere, and help to stimulate breeding behavior. .

Bony plates The relatively inflexible body covering associated with some fish, notably catfish, being present in place of **scales**.

Brackish Water conditions which are more saline than freshwater, but are not as salty as seawater. Typically encountered at the mouths of estuaries.

Bubblenest The floating nest created by male labyrinth fish using bubbles of saliva.

Cable tidy A connecting block that can take a number of electrical outputs from the aquarium and in turn joins to the main supply through a single plug.

Caudal fin The tail fin.

Chemical filtration Typically describes the use of activated carbon to remove harmful substances from solution.

Chromosomes The strands on which the genes are located in the nucleus of cells.

Condensation tray A barrier, often of perspex, between the aquarium and the hood, which prevents electrical connections becoming damp, and also slows loss of water from the tank.

Crown The center of a plant, from where new growth occurs.

Dechlorinator A product that removes harmful chlorine from local water supplies.

Dorsal fin The prominent fin which lies furthest forward on the upper area of the back.

Dropsy Abnormal swelling of the body. May have infectious or non-infectious causes.

Family A group of fish which consists of members of different **genera**.

Fancy A strain of fish selectively bred for characteristic features such as coloration or fin shape.

Filter bed The medium, such as gravel, through which water passes as part of the filtration process.

Flake Prepared food for fish which floats well on the water surface, being very thin.

Free-swimming The stage at which young fish start to swim around their quarters for the first time.

Fry Young fish.

Genus (Plural genera); a group of fish consisting of one or more **species**.

GH A measure of the general or permanent hardness of a water sample. Unaffected by boiling the water.

Gills The means by which fish extract oxygen from the water (though not the only means). Membranes well supplied with blood vessels located just behind the eyes on each side of the head.

Gonopodium The modified anal fin seen in various male **livebearers**, which is used for inseminating females.

Gravel tidy Sheet which fits on top of an under-gravel filter to prevent the slits becoming blocked in the substrate.

Gravid Describes the swollen appearance of female fish that indicates they are about to lay eggs or produce young.

Hard water Water that contains a relatively high level of dissolved calcium or magnesium salts.

Heaterstat Combined heater and thermostat unit for aquarium use.

KH A measure of temporary hardness, resulting from bicarbonates or carbonates dissolved in the water, which can be reduced by boiling.

Ichthyologists Those who study fish.

Labyrinth organ Auxiliary breathing organs located near to the gills, characteristic of labyrinth fish, which allows them to breathe atmospheric air directly.

Lateral line A sensory system running down the sides of the fish's body, allowing it to sense vibrations in the water.

Length Measurement of fish are usually carried out in a straight line from the snout to the base of the caudal fin, which is itself excluded from the figure.

Livebearers Fish that reproduce by means of internal fertilization, with females retaining their eggs in the body.

Mechanical filtration The direct removal of waste matter by filtration, sieving it out of the water.

Mouthbrooder A fish that retains its fertilized eggs in its mouth until they hatch, and may also allow its young back into its mouth for a period afterwards to escape danger.

Mulm The debris that can accumulate on the floor of the aquarium.

Nauplii The larval stage in the life-cycle of the brine shrimp *Artemia*, cultured as a rearing food for young fish.

New Tank Syndrome Describes the potential for sudden death of aquarium occupants resulting from a fatal build-up of ammonia and nitrite in a newly-established tank where the filtration system is not working effectively.

Nitrogen cycle The breakdown of toxic ammonia produced by the fish into nitrite and then less toxic nitrate, which is used by plants for growth.

Nocturnal Describes fish that are active after dark.

Operculum The movable flap that covers the **gills**, and allows water to flow over them.

Pectoral fin Paired fins located on each side of the body behind the **gills**.

Pelvic fin Fin present in front of the **anal fin**.

pH The relative **acidity** or **alkalinity** of a solution, based on a logarithmic scale, so each unit change represents a tenfold alteration in concentration, with pH 7 being neutral. Low values reflect increasing acidity: higher figures indicate a progressively more alkaline solution.

Pharyngeal teeth Sharp projections used for rasping food, located in the pharynx region of some fish at the back of the mouth.

Photosensitive Affected by light.

Photosynthesis Process by which plants manufacture their nutritional requirements using light.

Power filter A filtration unit that has its own pump to drive water through the unit.

Rays Bony framework that provides the structural support for the fins.

Scales Protective covering present over the bodies of most fish.

Soft water Water that is low in dissolved salts, includes most rainwater.

Spawning The process of mating and egg-laying.

Spawning mop Strands of material tied together to act as an artificial spawning site for those fish that typically spawn among roots rather than on the substrate.

Species A group of fish closely resembling each other that can interbreed and can produce fertile offspring.

Strain Line of fish specifically bred for particular characteristics such as color; may be named after the breeder responsible.

Substrate The floor covering in the aquarium or the base of the fish's natural habitat.

Surfactants Proteins, fats and other materials that rise to the top of water, creating a scum on the surface. Can be removed by a protein skimmer.

Swimbladder The fish's air-filled organ of buoyancy.

Taxonomy The science of identifying fish and unraveling their relationships.

Tomite The free-swimming, infective stage of the microscopic parasite that causes white spot.

Tubercles Slight swelling on the fins or body that characterizes male goldfish in breeding condition. Can sometimes be a symptom of illness too.

Undergravel filter A plate filter that fits right across the bottom of the aquarium.

Vent Ano-genital opening behind the anal fin.

Index

PICTURE CREDITS

Andromeda Oxford Limited 24t, 26x4, 102, 115, 116; Anthony & Elizabeth Bomford/Ardea 68; Mary Clay/Ardea 6; Nick Gordon/Ardea 86b; P. Morris/Ardea 42; John Dawes 7, 53; © www.Hippocampus-Bildarchiv.de. 2, 11–14b, 16, 19, 24b, 52, 58t, 60t, 61–64t, 69, 70l, 71l, 74l, 87, 88b, 91b, 96, 99; Max Gibbs/Photomax 9, 10b, 15, 16–17t, 20–23, 27–41, 46t–51, 55tl–57, 58b, 59, 60b, 64b–67, 70r, 71r–73, 74r, 75t–80, 82–86t, 88t, 89–91t, 92, 94–95, 97–98, 100, 101, 104–108, 110–113, 118–136b; M. Sandford 109; Peter Scoones/Science Photo Library 10t; Vitakraft Pet Products Co. Inc., New Jersey, U.S.A. 45, 114; Jane Burton/Warren Photographic 81, 93l, 93r.